Meet

Alien

Energy

with Dowsing

Susan Collins

Meet
Alien Energy
With Dowsing

Susan Collins

First Edition: June, 2016, ISBN: 978-0-9918300-2-2
Published by: Susan Joan Collins
335 Patricia Drive, King City, Ontario, L7B 1H4, Canada

Other books by Susan Collins

Bridge Matter and Spirit with Dowsing
Dowsing for Feng Shui and Space Clearing

In the **Dowsing that Works** series:

Use a Protocol to Get Results
Classic, Bible and Muslim Editions

Dowsing Triage
Finding and Fixing Energy Problems

Meeting Orbs in Sacred Space

Get Happy with Dowsing

Water Wells – What a Dowser Needs to Know

To order books, or arrange a workshop or personal session
contact Susan at **www.dowser.ca**
Books also available through Amazon

Testimonials for
Meet Alien Energy with Dowsing

"Susan's knowledge of Dowsing gives balance and a new perspective to the topic of Ufology. She gives you a way to find accurate information about Aliens and our interactions with them. Susan is a brilliant Speaker, Teacher and Dowser."

Jo-Anne Eadie
Director of Alien Cosmic Expo
www.aliencosmicexpo.com

"Susan has brought forward an important and timely dowsing system that works with the seen and unseen worlds that surround us. Delving into these topics with the right intentions will help us unlock hidden worlds of experience that will answer some of our most profound questions."

Jason Quitt
Author of "Forbidden Knowledge"
www.thecrystalsun.com

"Susan Collins is a well versed dowser and teacher. She is able to bring the art of dowsing to anyone interested in the topic. She explains the tools and protocols in ways that are demystifying yet encourage deeper exploration. Susan holds the broader vision of dowsing as a way to help the planet."

Adhi Moonien Two Owls
www.thenewglobalshaman.com

"Dowsing is an ancient method of communication that when used correctly in our modern society can reveal beneficial information to you. With Susan Collins as your dowsing guide, I have no doubt that you can develop the dowsing skill to access pertinent knowledge that will serve your personal growth."

Lana Marconi, Ph.D.
Director of THE RESONANCE film.
www.DrLana.com

Contents

1. **Introduction** ... 9

> How I feel down the metaphysical rabbit hole ... 10
> Structure of the book ...11

2. **Human beings and consciousness** ...13

> What it means to be human ...13
> Why are we here? Earth and Soul missions ...13
> Psychic Cords ...14
> Consciousness and perception ...14
> Multi-dimensional consciousness ...15
>> Déjà vu ...16
>> Simultaneous lives ...16
> Brainwave frequencies and consciousness ...17
> Resonance and electromagnetic fields ...18
> The God Helmet ...18
> Wi-Fi signals and paranormal activity ...19
> Sleep Paralysis and Alien abduction ...19
> Avoiding Sleep Paralysis ...20
> Lucid dreaming ...21

3. **Our Universe** ... 23

> The physics we know about ... 23
> The physics we don't know about ... 24
>> Dark energy and dark matter ... 25
>> The collapse of the quantum wave ... 25
> Light speed and Exoplanets ... 25
>> Distance between planets ... 26
>> Exoplanets ... 26

4. **Dowsing Fundamentals** ... 29

> How does dowsing work? ... 29
> Dowsing Tools ... 30
>> How to dowse with pendulums ...30
>> How to dowse with your body ... 31
> The Dowsing Protocol ... 31
>> The Dowsing Protocol summary ... 33
> What if your pendulum doesn't work? ... 35
> Practice ... 36

5. **Create Psychic Protection** ... 39
Techniques to manage Alien interaction ... 40
   Stay in control ... 40
   Don't allow Alien Beings to name themselves ...41
   Get help from the Beneficial Beings ... 42
   The Dowsing Protocol ... 42
      Disconnect Alien interference ... 42
      Create and maximize health ... 44
   Affirmations ... 45
   Emotional Freedom Technique ... 46
   Reprogram the experience ... 47
   The Dream Time ... 47
   Ceremony ... 48
   Find Community ... 48
   Physical protection versus energy remedies ... 48
      Give the problem form, then destroy it ... 49
   The last resort ... 49

6. **Dowse about Alien Beings** ... 51
A brief history of Aliens ... 51
The evidence ... 53
How do Aliens get here ... 53
   Portals ... 53
What do Aliens look like ... 54
   Orb shape shifters ...54
   The uncanny valley ... 55
Do Alien Beings speak English? ... 56
Why don't more Alien beings contact Humans? ... 57
Why do Alien Beings want to come to Earth? ...57
Spirit Guides, Walk-ins, Star Children etc. ... 58
Beneficial, Nonbeneficial and Neutral Alien Beings ... 58
   Don't make a deal with the devil ... 58
Resonance and "Divine Holy Love" ... 60
Can Alien beings get stuck here? ... 60
Alien Energy Survey ... 61

7. **Dowse about you and Alien Beings** ... 65
Close Encounters ... 66
Encountering your Self as an Alien Being ... 67

8. **Dowse your other energy experiences** ... 71

Encountering Non-Human, Non-Alien beings … 71
Are you creating the experience? … 71
Where does the energy experience originate? … 74

9. **Initiating Contact with Alien Beings** … 75
More techniques to manage Alien interaction … 76
Interact as equals … 76
Interview with an Alien … 77
Helping Beneficial Beings … 78

10. **Conclusion** … 81

Appendix: Preliminary Survey Results …82
Glossary … 84
Bibliography … 88
About the author … 89
Susan's books … 90

Tables

Table 1: States of Consciousness … 15
Table 2: Brainwave frequency and functions … 17
Table 3: Exoplanets in our area of the Milky Way … 26
Table 4: Known Exoplanet distances from Earth … 27
Table 5: Close Encounter Classifications … 66
Table 6: Known Exoplanet distances from Earth . . 27

Boxes

Box 1: Living simultaneous lives … 17
Box 2: A child's ghost story … 41
Box 3: Thought Experiment One: Change the memory … 47
Box 4: Algon and the Sky Girl … 52
Box 5: Alien Orbs … 55
Box 6: Bill and Archangel Michael at the hot tub … 60
Box 7: Thought Experiment Two: Creating the future … 76

Surveys

Survey 1: Practice dowsing questions … 37
Survey 2: Am I ready to dowse safely about Alien Beings? … 62
Survey 3: Dowse about Alien Beings … 63
Survey 4: Dowse about you and Alien beings …67
Survey 5: Dowse about You and your experience … 69

Survey 6: I AM creating this Energy Experience … 72
Survey 7: I am NOT creating this Energy Experience … 73
Survey 8: Where does the Energy Experience originate? … 74
Survey 9: Determine if Beneficial or Nonbeneficial Being … 77
Survey 10: Interview with a Beneficial Being … 78
Survey 11: Can you help the Beneficial Being … 79

Thanks to

Harry, Harrison and Jocelyn Dahme
for inspiring my life

Jo-Anne Eadie and Lana Marconi
for ramping up the discussion

and to my all my teachers and colleagues
who have shared the journey so far

1 Introduction

"To my mathematical brain, the numbers alone make thinking about aliens perfectly rational. The real challenge is to work out what aliens might actually be like."
Stephen Hawking
*Author and Professor at Cambridge**

Late one night a few years ago I was leading a workshop on orb photography at a conference in Salmon Arm beside Lake Shuswap, a typically isolated town in central British Columbia, Canada. I'd run the workshop many times before in different places and knew that it was easiest for beginners to get clear pictures of Orbs** if the sky was dark and there were no streetlights. We'd talked about orbs during the class and how to communicate with their energies and how to safely invite them to be photographed.

I was confident that the cloudless, still night on the dark lake would be the perfect setting. I was dismayed when I pushed open the heavy doors of our building to bring our group outside to begin the photo session to see that there were search lights flashing down from the sky sweeping across the silent water. My first emotion was irritation – the Orb photo session would be ruined by helicopters! My mind caught up to my emotion when I noticed there was no sound, wind or disturbance on the water. It couldn't be a helicopter. As the question *"Where are the lights coming from"* began to form in my mind, they vanished. I turned to the people around me and asked if they'd seen the lights. *"YES"* one responded, and others nodded. *"We get a lot of UFOs here"*

**Steven Hawking is the Dennis Stanton Avery and Sally Tsui Wong-Avery Director of Research at the Department of Applied Mathematics and Theoretical Physics and Founder of the Centre for Theoretical Cosmology at Cambridge*

*** See Glossary page 84 for definitions.*

There had been no visible source of the light display and I had no logical explanation as to where the lights had come from. Had I really just had a UFO experience? I have no other explanation and have continued to study energy phenomena, metaphysics (the nature of reality) and have come to some conclusions about Aliens and UFO phenomena that I would like to share in this book.

How I fell down the metaphysical rabbit hole

As a Personal Management Consultant and Professional Dowser my job is to help people make sense of extraordinary events in their lives by assisting them in accessing levels of consciousness that are not normally available to them. How do I know how to do this? Because from earliest childhood I have personally experienced many paranormal events that have set me on a mission to try and understand them and explain their origin.

As a child I felt there were ghosts everywhere and thought that they were out to get me. I dreamed of black figures hovering over my bed. I noticed that when I thought about things they often happened. I also, seriously, wondered why I was not a chair or a mountain and why the people around me were my family Déjà vu episodes were an everyday occurrence.

Perhaps all children have those thoughts and experiences, but nobody talked about those things when I was growing up in the 50's and 60's.

As a young adult I applied to Canada's first astronaut program even though I had no academic or other qualifications for the job. I received a pleasant letter of rejection, but never gave up my dream of travelling into space. Needless to say I was a fan of *Star Trek* and *Star Wars* and *Doctor Who*.

I looked for answers in many dusty corners on my quest to explain the unusual things I was experiencing (and also in an effort to recover from rheumatoid arthritis which crippled my hands and knees when I was 29 – but that's another story.)

The most useful tool I found on this journey has been dowsing which is a simple biofeedback device that allows me to interact with subtle energies in my environment. Dowsing can be used to find energies that are not detectable with our standard five senses: touch, taste, smell, sight and sound.

My mission now is to share what I've learned and to make exploration of the paranormal normal. To show people how to discover, through direct experience, the mechanisms of the multi-dimensional universe and to help them find answers to the questions that drive them.

Structure of the Book

Whether or not you have ever dowsed before, this book will give you a way to find out more about Alien Beings and their interactions with humans.

The first part of the book provides background information on **Human Beings and Consciousness** (page 13) and **Our Universe** (page 23). These sections will help you understand how our states of consciousness may affect our experience of Alien presence as well as the phenomena of Alien abduction. You will discover that maintaining conscious awareness will increase your personal control over all events and interactions.

The science overview touches on what is known about the physical universe and suggests that Alien Beings may originate and travel through interdimensional portals.

Dowsing Fundamentals (page 29) explains that accurate dowsing can be a powerful tool because it is easy to learn, and with practice and the use of Dowsing Protocols, you can discover a great deal about your Self and the world around you.

The "sixth sense", the one we use to dowse, is based on electromagnetic energy. Humans, like many creatures, are able to both emit and detect variable electromagnetic states. Even if you've never felt particularly intuitive before, if you're drawn to know about Alien Beings, you are ready to find out more, and dowsing is your ticket to knowledge.

Before beginning your investigation you'll need to **Create Psychic Protection** (page 39). Once you are confident in your ability to dowse accurately and be safe while you're doing it, it will be time to **Dowse About Alien Beings** (page 51), **Dowse about you and Alien Beings** (page 65), and **Dowse about your other energy experiences** (page 71).

If you are confident in your abilities, you can take the step of **Initiating Contact with Alien Beings** (page 75). But PLEASE take the time to read through the rest of the book before you jump in at the deep end, even if you are already a seasoned dowser. There are many things we don't know and it's much easier to be prepared for all eventualities before starting your journey.

The **Conclusion** of this book (page 81) is certainly not the end of the discussion on dowsing for Alien Beings and energy. Please send me the results of your Surveys (page 82), and if you are willing, your personal stories about Alien interactions, and I will include them in future editions of this book.

2. Human Beings and Consciousness

"I regard consciousness as fundamental. I regard matter as derivative from consciousness.
Everything that we talk about, everything that we regard as existing, postulates consciousness."
Max Planck, Nobel Prize Winner in Physics, 1918
for his work on quantum theory

What it means to be Human

Before we talk about Alien energy, we'd better talk about what it means to be a Human and the levels of consciousness we experience. We'll also need to know something about accepted physics to be able to understand how it's even possible for Alien energy to show up on our planet. And we'd better know something about the structure of our known universe so we can make informed speculations about what else is out there.

A healthy human has a balanced body, mind, emotions, intellect and energy. We need to balance all these aspects into a unified package to stay healthy. If the physical body dies, then we die. If our emotional body dies then we can't function. If any aspect of our bodies weakens or dies then we can't function as healthy human beings.

Proper nutrition, exercise and rest are important to support our physical functions, but we need to seek health in all parts of our beings including the parts of ourselves that we tend to hide from people. To be healthy we need to admit that there are parts that aren't happy, that are afraid, that are jealous, that are greedy; what popular culture calls the "dark" side. Psychologist Carl Jung called this "embracing the shadow". For the purposes of this book, embracing the shadow means finding the courage to look directly at some of the things that may scare us or that we are afraid may be true or that we want to be true. It means putting aside the ego and simply asking for the truth.

Why are we here? Earth and Soul missions

Philosophers have filled libraries trying to answer the question of why are we here, both as a species on the planet and as individuals within the short span of our lives. We may not all agree on the "why" but I suggest that while we're here, we have things we are meant to do, and that if we do them, our lives run more smoothly. I'm referring to Earth missions, such as earning a living and feeding our own families, and Soul missions, which are generally service-based, broader in nature, (such as helping out in areas of disaster where there is no personal reward) and that may extend over different incarnations.

It may be that uncompleted Earth and Soul Missions create Psychic Cords (see below) between ourselves, other people and even Alien Beings that persist through our various incarnations. Although outdated vows and commitments sound like chains that bind us through eternity, it is possible to disconnect them using the Dowsing Protocol (page 31).

Psychic Cords

Psychic Cords are energy connections between people, places, animals and, potentially, Alien Beings. Beneficial Psychic Cords are naturally formed between parents and young children and ensure the survival of our species, however they are meant to dissolve as children become independent. Nonbeneficial cords are created when the energy connections don't naturally fall away, or when an adult becomes attached to something or someone in an unhealthy way. Nonbeneficial Psychic Cords are characterised by a personal loss of energy.

Cords are sometimes created when personal or business relationships end with unresolved issues. People may stay connected through jealousy, longing, anger or other strong unresolved emotion. It's as if the energy of one person is being sucked out by the other. Psychic cords can last through many life times and it may be that some of us have Psychic Cords tying us to Alien Beings due to unresolved issues relating to previous Soul Missions.

Consciousness and perception

Humans learn to make quick choices based on the available facts. We are good at pattern recognition because that was an essential skill of our ancestors both as hunters, and to avoid being hunted. We needed to know if a rustle in the grass and the dark shape behind it was a bush or a bear. We needed to be able to make quick decisions and act on them. Our gut reactions weren't always right, but we tended to act on them.

We modern humans tend to have more time for considered reasoning in our everyday lives. Except for driving, and Mixed Martial Artists, our survival doesn't depend so much on reaction time. However, just as for our ancestors, our minds often get made up in that first split second of an experience. The saying *"You only have one chance to make a first impression"* is relevant here, but we must remember that a careful review of the facts and chance to mull things over can bring a richer view of the world. We are stubborn though, and it is sometimes as difficult to change our own minds as it is to change someone else's. Our sense of Self is often tied to being right, and it can seem like a loss of personal power to admit that one's first impression was not entirely right.

The human characteristic of making snap judgments and sticking with them does not necessarily serve us well when we experience phenomena that we haven't seen before or do not understand. For early humans, an eclipse of the sun was a potentially world ending event that they believed only supplication to their gods could prevent. For some, unexplained lights in the sky or unusually vivid dreams could be interpreted as proof of Alien presence.

Much of how we see and interpret the world depends on our states of consciousness while we are having the experience of something. In the simplest sense, we see different things when we are awake than when we are asleep or when we are consciously focused or passively aware.

Somewhere inside our body-mind-spirit system of thoughts, emotions and experiences, we find different levels of consciousness that determine how we see and interpret the world. Knowing about this is important when we are discussing Aliens and interactions with them. It seems likely that if we are experiencing interactions with Aliens that we are in an altered state of consciousness. In fact, being in an altered state of consciousness may be prerequisite to interaction with Alien Beings!

Generally accepted states of consciousness follow.

Table 1: States of Consciousness

Mind State	Characteristics
Conscious mind	everything inside our "normal", waking awareness. Easy to access.
Preconscious mind	memories and information that can be easily retrieved by the conscious mind.
Unconscious mind	reservoir of feelings, thoughts and urges outside of our conscious minds but that we can recall at will.
Subconscious mind	existing in the mind but not consciously known or felt and difficult to access.
Super-conscious mind	transcending human consciousness, and accessing a reservoir of knowledge. Difficult to access.

Multi-dimensional consciousness

There are forms of consciousness that don't fit neatly into the categories above. The experience of Déjà Vu, Simultaneous Lives and Psychic Cords are examples.

Deja Vu

"Deja vu" means "already seen" in French. The literature will tell you that Deja Vu experiences (the conviction that you have already experienced in the past a sequence of events that you are experiencing in the current moment) are related to epilepsy.

I don't have epilepsy, but I have often had these experiences. The most extreme example in my case occurred several decades ago. I woke from a vivid nightmare in which I worked in an office and had been having a long technical discussion with my coworkers about graphic design, using words I didn't know the meaning of. The dream ended with me promising to complete an assignment which I knew I didn't know how to do. I panicked and woke up.

Years later I became a graphic designer and one day the nightmare played itself out in my reality. The same office, the same people, the same words and the same assignment. But at this point in my life, I understood the job and how to do it, and when I committed to complete the project, I was able to do so.

My own theory of how Déjà Vu is created, is that since time and space are bent by mass (see Einstein page 23), Deja Vu experiences are caused by the bending of space-time, due to the presence of theoretical, microscopic black holes that can somehow present in our dimension. Perhaps we only perceive this warping of time when we are in a certain state of consciousness, perhaps while sleeping, so the experience of the future is experienced as a dream. Those who remember their dreams have the chance to glimpse the future.

Simultaneous lives

The sense of experiencing simultaneous lives, probably accessed through a superconscious level of mind, is more common than one would think. If, however, someone went to a doctor and described their sensations, they would probably be diagnosed with a mental illness and put on medication. It is out of fear of being misunderstood and ridiculed that most people with the awareness of other realities do not reveal them. My colleague Jason Quitt, author of *"Forbidden Knowledge"* has been fearless in speaking out on this topic.

Levi G., a colleague who constantly seeks balance between the demands of his Earth mission and the awareness of his Soul mission, describes below how normal it is for him to have the feeling of living multiple simultaneous lives. For people who have this awareness, it is important for them to remember to focus on their Earth missions and not to be distracted by the perception of other existences. For those with advanced abilities in perception, it may be possible to access these other realities and to bring useful information back into standard reality in order to integrate the missions.

Box 1: Living simultaneous lives

Living simultaneous lives

"For most of my life I have sensed my existence in other dimensions, planes and time frames. It feels like I am living a full life in more than one place or time, as if there are more than one "me" but it is still "me".

Have you ever lived in a house or apartment where there are other people in the building, moving about? To me, I can feel my other existences similar to the way one can feel other people or beings that are nearby.

Sometimes I sense that my other existences and experiences are occurring at the same time, but in another dimension, and other times it feels more like they are occurring in other time frames. It all seems very normal and makes sense to me."   Levi G

Brainwave frequencies and consciousness

Different levels of consciousness are related to different brain wave frequencies. Brain waves are recorded in cycles per second (Hertz / Hz,) and traditionally correspond to the following activities:

Table 2: Brainwave frequency and functions

Name	Hertz	Function
Gamma	32	Multi-sensory processing
Beta	16 - 31	"Normal" waking
Alpha	8 – 15	Relaxation
Theta	4 – 7	Dreaming, meditation
Delta	Less than 4	Loss of body awareness

With practice, individuals can move through these states at will, and research has shown that the brains of active dowsers can simultaneously operate within the full range of frequencies. The advantage of this is that dowsers can establish and maintain links between different states of consciousness, take discerning action within them and then remember events that occur within those states of consciousness!

Clearly this is a handy skill for finding out more about Aliens if much of our interaction with them is occurring in altered states of consciousness.

For people who believe they may have experienced Alien abduction or interference, training the brain to be alert in all frequencies is the first step in being an active player in the situation. The most powerful tool we have is our free will. I often say this is the Free Will planet, and it may be we have come here simply to learn how to make choices. When we are consciously engaged in a situation we may find the power to change it. If we can maintain our conscious awareness, we are better able to make choices and can choose to defend ourselves against all types of interference.

In my practice I have found that some groups of Alien Beings do not want to interact with a Human that is asking questions. It seems that some groups have a "hive mind" that runs best when all members submit their individual will to the group. Having a pesky Human who questions the authority of the group can be too much trouble for the hive and the Alien group itself backs off.

Resonance and electromagnetic fields

We are able to perceive things we are resonant with. That means that if practice modulating our brain wave frequencies, we will be able to perceive more things.

Dowsers detect the electromagnetic frequencies of various things – everything from moving water to moving ghosts. You may have already experienced flickering lights as an indicator of Spirit presence. (It isn't always, but once you know how to dowse, when the lights flicker, you can ask: *"Is that a communication from Spirit."* If so, you can use your dowsing ability to find out what the communication is. It is my experience that once you confront the phenomena head on, it is much easier to resolve issues.

Conscious energies (such as ghosts) attempting communications don't often go away if we ignore them, typically they get more intense (as in the case of poltergeists who just want someone to pay attention as well as those mischievous energies who keep taking your glasses and putting them back in a place you've already looked.)

We are mixing up the words "other-dimensional beings", "Aliens" and "Spirits" because it is often hard to tell them apart. Some things come from this planet, some don't. The series of questions you'll be dowsing later will help you tell the difference between them. The point is, that not all unusual phenomena are caused by Aliens or Spirits, some are simply caused by electromagnetic fluctuations in appliances and power grids.

The God Helmet

The "God Helmet" is the informal name given to a device developed by Stan Koren and Dr. Michael Persinger of Laurentian University in Canada, which they refer to as the Koren Helmet.

The Koren helmet manipulates electromagnetic fields in the temporal lobes of the brain of the person wearing it so that they experience differences in their brain wave frequencies. This often results in their experience of a variety of phenomena some of which include a sense of another presence in the room and other mystical experiences.

The Koren Helmet appears to demonstrate that fluctuating magnetic fields may alter one's brain wave frequencies and could create the experience of Alien presence.

Wi-Fi signals and paranormal activity

Whether fluctuating electromagnetic frequencies in our environment simulate paranormal activity or in fact stimulate them, we need to know about what is happening around us before we jump to conclusions about either Aliens lurking in the corners of our bedroom or ghosts hiding in the closet. For example, if you live close to an airport you are being subjected to regular radar pulses that may overstimulate your brain on a regular basis and could cause perceptual distortions.

We are surrounded by fluctuating electromagnetic fields through power grids, Wi-Fi, portable phones and a many other devices we have come to rely on. The Earth itself has a strong electromagnetic field, and differences in the electrical charge between the Earth and the Sky can create strong disturbances. (Think of any scary movie from Frankenstein to Star Wars, and there will generally be electromagnetic discharges signalling the presence of something bad.

If we don't know there is an electromagnetic fluctuation, we may attribute the sensations we experience to an outside cause so we need to be discerning and investigate all possible causes.

Sleep Paralysis and Alien abduction

Some people describe waking up at night in their beds and being unable to move. This may be combined with the feeling that there is something or someone else, such as an Alien, in the room with them and may include the sensation of being attacked or manipulated by that being.

The medical literature describes this as Sleep Paralysis and that it may occur in the half awake state, either when falling asleep or when waking up. During the dream state, the brain emits chemicals to immobilize the muscles so we don't thrash around in our sleep. If the brain wakes up before the body, then Sleep Paralysis may occur.

It may be that in that half awake state when sleep paralysis occurs, our changing brain wave frequencies (see above) give us access to different levels of information and consciousness that we do not normally experience.

In many cultures it is believed that the paralysis is caused by supernatural beings physically interacting with them. The experience may include buzzing and the feeling of being dragged out of bed. Experiencers, people who feel they have unwillingly interacted with Aliens, describe exactly this, and it is very often a frightening one for them.

To dismiss the experience of Alien interaction as a by-product of Sleep Paralysis underestimates the complexity of our multi-frequency and multi-dimensional universe. We must ask ourselves whether paranormal activity is being simulated or stimulated. If it feels real is it real? Maybe.

As a child I would sense black shapes hovering over me in bed just a few inches from my face. Terrified, I would physically throw myself out of bed and end up in a heap on the floor. Apparently my "Flight" response (as opposed to a "Fight) response overcame any sleep paralysis I may have had.

For the record, I dreamt of fearful black shapes and demons until I had the courage to face them while I was conscious. Over time, I realized that rather than these things being out to get me, they generally wanted me to help them. Through dowsing (and always using the Dowsing Protocol for safety), I now dialogue regularly with a range of beings I cannot see. It's a bit like the internet – we may not be able to see the person who sends us an email, but we treat them as real.

Avoiding Sleep Paralysis

While some people may enjoy the opportunity to journey through different states of consciousness, many would prefer just to get a good night's sleep and to use other forms of mind control to access altered states of awareness.

Some say you can avoid sleep paralysis by avoiding napping during the day, by getting enough sleep at night and by not sleeping on your back.

If you find yourself in paralysis, you can try to get out of it in a variety of ways. First, remember that sleep paralysis is a natural transition between sleeping and waking. Prepare an affirmation such as: *"My body is asleep and I'm ok. I'm going to wake up now"*. Decide to fully wake up and relax your body by breathing deeply. If you can, move small muscles on purpose to wake up. Most of the "paralysis" is in the belly, chest and throat areas, so it may be easier to move your fingers and toes as a way of regaining control.

Or you can trigger a flight response that immediately wakes you up on high alert.

Lucid Dreaming

If you have been practicing dowsing or doing other types of personal mind control, you can stay fully conscious while you are dreaming and in a state of Sleep Paralysis. As a lucid dreamer you can retain your power and use your free will to choose what happens next. If you want to banish these experiences from your life you can do so. If you want to more fully engage with them, you can do so, but on terms that you negotiate.

To begin to lucid dream, simply tell yourself as you are falling asleep that you will:

- remember your dreams
- that you will be aware of any danger around you
- that you will wake up if you want to
- that you can control the dream
- that you are safe

You will read more about creating psychic protection in Chapter 4.

22

3 Our Universe

"The fact that religions through the ages have spoken in images, parables, and paradoxes means simply that there are no other ways of grasping the reality to which they refer."

Neils Bohr
Nobel Prize in Physics, 1922.

The world contains things that we don't perceive with our normal five senses of taste, sight, touch, hearing and smell. There is a sixth sense as well – it is the ability to detect and transmit electromagnetic energy.

We know this to be true because many of our modern medical diagnostic machines such as MRIs and ECG's analysis our body's electromagnetic signatures to determine our health.

Our bodies themselves are piezoelectric and can detect subtle changes in electromagnetic fluctuation (as can the bodies of other creatures). The science behind the dowsing response phenomena is based on the human body's natural ability to detect subtle changes in the electromagnetic field.

The physics we know about

Metaphysics is the study of the nature of reality and any book that has dowsing and Aliens as its primary themes is certainly a book on metaphysics. But before we go too far into the unknown physics of the universe that brings us interactions with Alien life forms, let's do a brief survey of physics over the last three hundred years to review what we generally understand about how our physical world operates.

Sir Isaac Newton: The Clockwork Universe (1642-1727)

Modern physics more or less starts with Sir Isaac Newton who described a "Clockwork Universe" wherein objects move uniformly. He also supplied us with theories of energy, motion and gravity.

Albert Einstein: The Relative Universe (1879-1955)

Albert Einstein received the Nobel Prize in Physics in 1921 for his "services to theoretical physics". He described theories of General Relativity which included the expected properties of the universe on a large scale. He predicted the overall curvature of the universe, curved space time and (recently recorded) gravity waves. He stated that the laws of physics are the same for everyone in uniform motion and that matter and energy curve both space and time (**Space-time**). He also said that time runs slower in areas of strong gravity (where Space-time is tightly curved), that gravity bends light and that things compress in the direction of motion.

He predicted the presence of Alien life: *"Why should the earth be the only planet supporting human life? It is not singular in any other respect."*

Neils Bohr: The Quantum Enigma (1885-1962)

Neils Bohr was a champion of Quantum physics which describes the physics of things at a microscopic level. He, and others, described energy as being delivered in discreet packets, or quanta and asked if energy behaved as particles or waves. Quantum physicists noticed that if they observed an action, they affected it, so that the observer becomes part of the equation.

Werner Heisenberg: String theory (1901-1976)

Werner Heisenberg and many modern researchers have worked on the theory that the fundamental entities of matter are not particles but tiny, string-like loops and that there are 11 dimensions (as opposed to the normal three plus time that we think of as our everyday dimensions). In string theory, the 11 dimensions don't extend forever like the "normal" dimensions. They are curled up into vibrating, tiny closed structures.

We don't have much direct contact with these 11 dimensions, but for the purposes of this book, it does give us a place where Alien life forms might be existing along side of us.

The physics we don't know about

As much as we know about the physical universe, there is far more that we don't know or haven't proven. Without proof, theoretical physics is a form of science fiction. As author Arthur C. Clarke famously said, *"Any sufficiently advanced technology is indistinguishable from magic"*. At this writing for example, neither "black holes" (dense matter with a very strong gravitational field) nor "wormholes" (a connection between widely separated points in space) have been proven, though at least the effect of black holes has been observed.

Continued research will no doubt eventually result in answers to many puzzles, perhaps including how Alien Beings could use interdimensional transport to visit our Earth dimensions.

Dark energy and dark matter

Scientists currently don't know what dark matter and dark energy are – just that they are active forces and make up 95% of the known universe.

They are hypothetical forms of matter and energy invisible to electromagnetic radiation that account for gravitational forces observed in the universe. NASA indicates that roughly 68% of the Universe is dark energy. Dark matter makes up about 27%. The rest, everything on Earth, everything ever observed with all of our instruments, all normal matter, adds up to less than 5% of the Universe!

There's a lot we don't know about the cosmos, and there's a lot we don't understand at the micro level as well. Scientists used to refer to the 98.8% of DNA they didn't understand as "junk" or "garbage" DNA. The more enlightened term used now is "noncoding" DNA, but we still don't understand what it's doing. As above, so below: there are many mysteries to solve!

The collapse of the quantum wave

The reality we perceive is the collapse of the quantum wave of possibilities. What does that mean? We'd need to have degrees in quantum physics to fully explain or understand it, but roughly, everything is made up of "stuff" that is made up of both waves and particles depending on how you observe and measure the 'stuff'. All things are possible until they are observed, acted upon or in fact intended.

Once the "stuff" is observed, the particle precipitates into reality where the quantum wave of possibilities is strongest (where our attention is greatest). In every-day language, we can say that our thoughts create our reality and refer to the collapse of the quantum wave as the Law of Attraction. Einstein called it *"spooky action at a distance."* To take an extreme view, we could say that since all matter was connected at the moment of the Big Bang, all things can be influenced now through our intention.

Light Speed and Exoplanets

When I was growing up I was taught that Earth was the only habitable planet and there were no planets outside of our Solar System.

I was also taught that humans were the only creatures to use tools. Today we know that both those things are wrong. And there's a lot more we don't about, such as "dark" energy and matter.

Distance between planets: Light Years

Let's go back to conventional physics and consider the size of space. Let's say we find some lovely exoplanets that Humans might like to travel to or that Aliens might come from. How far away are those places, and how long would it take to get there?

The vast distances of space are generally measured in Light Years, the distance that light travels in one year: 9 trillion kilometres (6 trillion miles) at a speed of 300,000 kilometers (186,000 miles) per second. There's not much in our human scale to compare that speed to, but, at this writing, New Horizons (the Pluto mission craft) is the fastest launched object with a cruising speed of about 45 km (28 miles) per second. You can do the math on that, but the message is, it would take a human craft more than one lifetime to get most places.

Stephen Hawking says *"I think it quite likely that we are the only civilization within several hundred light years; otherwise we would have heard radio waves."* Of course this statement assumes that Alien Beings would be generating radio waves. However even if it is true, we cannot discount the possibility that civilizations further away from that may have devised a method of interstellar or inter-dimensional transport that we have no knowledge of.

Exoplanets

NASA has two missions, Kepler and K2, that are surveying our region of the Milky Way for Earth-size and smaller planets in or near the (human) habitable zone, to determine how many stars in our galaxy might have such planets. Planets outside of our solar system are called Exoplanets.

At the time of writing, MANY planets have been found to have Earth-like conditions.

Table 3: Exoplanets in our area of the Milky Way

(Accurate as of June 2016. MANY more have been discovered since then.)

Planets found	Kepler	K2	Total
Candidates	4,302	270	4572
Confirmed	1,284	39	1323
Small habitable zone confirmed	12	NA	12

Paul Hertz, the Astrophysics Division director at NASA Headquarters says *"We now know there could be more planets than stars,"* Of course many of these planets are too far away for us to get to (see Table 4) and we don't yet have a viable concept for how other life forms could travel across the distance required to get to Earth.

As exciting as it is to find out about habitable-zone exoplanets, its' important to remember that these surveys are only considering places that could potentially support human life. If we are investigating Aliens, we must take into account that it is quite probable that many Alien species would have different physical requirements to support their life.

Table 4: Known Exoplanet distances from Earth
(Accurate as of June 2016. MANY more plenets been discovered since then.)

Known Planets	Distance away in light years
Gliese 674b	14.8
3	within 20
11	within 30
21	within 40

The closest star system (Alpha Centauri) is 4.1 light-years away. Let's put that distance on a scale we can imagine. Imagine that the distance between the Earth and the Sun distance was 1 meter (3.3 feet). If that was the case, the distance between Earth and Alpha Centauri from Earth would be 271 kilometers (169 miles). That's about the distance between Toronto and North Bay, or New York and Baltimore or London and Manchester.

In any case, as Stephen Hawking points out *"We think that life develops spontaneously on Earth, so it must be possible for life to develop on suitable planets elsewhere in the universe. But we don't know the probability that a planet develops life."*

So perhaps the Alien beings don't necessarily originate exclusively from "out there". The truth may be wrapped up in other dimensions right here on Earth! (See String theory page 23) There are probably more habitable zones that would support Alien life than we can count!

28

4 Dowsing Fundamentals

Dowsing is the detection and transformation of energy with simple tools and the power of heart and thought. It has always been known as a way to find water and minerals, but today modern dowsers also use their skills to detect, and interact with physical, mental, emotional, spiritual energies and even Alien energies.

The ability to dowse is a natural, sensory ability we all have. It is not based on a religious practice, but I find the best results come when I align myself with the "Divine Source".

To get the results you want it is important to use a Dowsing Protocol (page 31) every time you dowse. No dowser is one hundred percent accurate all the time, but I guarantee that using this protocol every time you dowse will increase your accuracy and provide protection. Your level of accuracy can drop off if you are tired, hungry, intoxicated or sick.

If you don't use a Dowsing Protocol before you dowse you leave yourself wide open to psychic attack. (See Psychic Protection page 39)

How Does Dowsing Work?

Our bodies have natural electromagnetic receptors, so with practice we can learn to sense and interpret subtle energies. It is similar to our ability to sort out different audio frequencies to identify different types of music. Dowsers use tools to amplify these subtle signals in their bodies.

The key to all successful dowsing is to make sure your thoughts are focused, and that your questions are clear. It is also important to stay emotionally detached from the outcome, even though the answers may be very important to you and may trigger emotional responses. The Dowsing Protocol helps you stay objective. Chapters 6 to 9 contain many surveys to which you can dowse the answers, however your answers will have no meaning if your dowsing is not accurate.If you are

Practice dowsing accurately before you begin the surveys! If you are a new dowser, work with a pendulum and the Dowsing Protocol on practice questions before beginning the questions in Chapters 6 to 9.

a new dowser, work with a pendulum and the Dowsing Protocol on practice questions before beginning the surveys.

Dowsing Tools

Anything that moves can be a dowsing tool. The common tools are: pendulums (any weighted object on a string); L-rods (bent wires); Y-rods (forked sticks); and your fingers. The tools themselves have no magic power, just as a hammer has no power to drive a nail until we pick it up. The tools simply amplify our body's sensory perceptions. Learning to use the tools is easy. Learning to relax and focus your mind at the same time takes practice.

In this book I will teach you how to dowse with a pendulum and your fingers – that's all you need to know to dowse about Aliens. (*Please see my other books for more discussion of how to use tools.*)

How to dowse with pendulums

The basic movements of the pendulum are: swinging back and forth, (either away from you, or across your body), and swinging in circles (clockwise or counter clockwise). There are other subtle movements that you will begin to recognize as you develop a personal vocabulary.

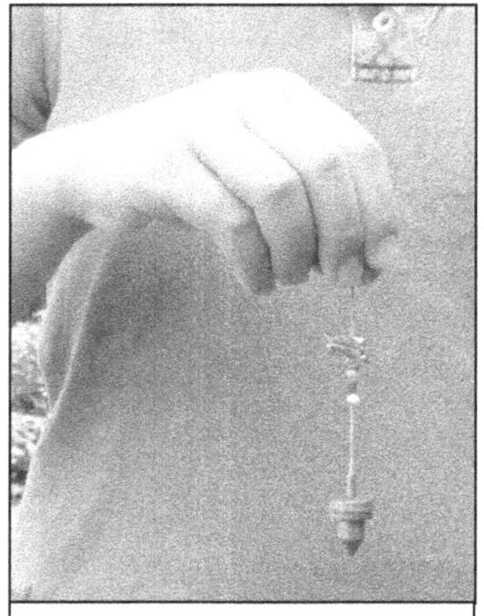

Anything that swings freely can be used a dowsing pendulum.

The first step is to determine what YOUR responses mean. Your responses may be different from another person's. This is how to program your responses (and this is the only step where you will consciously be asking the pendulum to move in certain directions):

- Hold the string between your thumb and first finger, about 10 cm (4 inches) from the weight at the end (see diagram). While slowly swinging the pendulum back and forth, say out loud *"Pendulum, show me YES"*. The pendulum should move.
- If there is no response, swing the pendulum clockwise for a few seconds (if that is what you'd like your YES response to be), and say: *"Pendulum this is my YES."* Then repeat the question *"Pendulum, show me my YES."* Keep doing this until the pendulum moves on its

own. This step creates the brain map that helps your body to amplify subconscious information.

- Repeat these steps for NO, DISCONNECT (used in Step 4 of the Protocol) and MAXIMIZE responses (used in Step 5).
- Practice until you are comfortable with your answers.

What do the different motions mean?

For many people the YES response is a back and forth (towards and away from the body) motion. For others YES is a clockwise, circular spin. NO for many people is a continuous left-right-left swing across the body; for others it is a counter-clockwise spin. Practice until you can reliably recognize your own YES and NO answers.

For many people the DISCONNECT signal (used in Step 4 of the Dowsing Protocol to remove non-beneficial energy) is a counter-clock wise spin and the MAXIMIZE signal (Step 5, increase beneficial energy) is a clockwise spin.

Once you recognize your YES and NO responses, let the pendulum give the responses on its own when you ask questions or work with energies. Start the pendulum swinging gently in a neutral direction (an angle slightly off centre), state your intention (or ask your questions), then let the pendulum respond naturally. Ask for well location, depth and volume.

How to dowse with Your body

There are simple methods for getting a dowsing response just by using your body. Make an "O" with the thumb and fore finger of one hand and try to pull them apart with the thumb and fore finger of the other hand. While you're doing this, ask *"Show me YES"*, then *"Show me NO"*. Generally your YES will be the one that is more difficult to pull apart.

The Dowsing Protocol

When you begin as a dowser you might wonder if you're just fooling yourself when the pendulum moves one way or another. You may not trust your answers. The Dowsing Protocol below will guide you through the steps to truly develop your intuition so that you can trust the answers you get with dowsing.

To get accurate results, use a Dowsing Protocol every time you dowse. This practice will help you "zone in" to the energies that are affecting your state of happiness. It will also provide protection from all sources of non-beneficial energy and influence.

If you don't use the Protocol or some other sort of energy management and protection system before you dowse, it would be like picking up the phone, dialling random numbers, and taking advice from whoever answered. If you do zone in with a Protocol before you dowse, you'll get your answers from the "Divine Source" (or however you address your highest spiritual principle), and the answers will be more accurate. With the Protocol you will never be given more energy or information than you can handle.

The Dowsing Protocol I'm sharing with you below may seem like a lot of trouble to go through, but if you use it before each session, your accuracy will increase. If you do the first five steps of it several times a day, even when you're not dowsing for wells, you may find that you experience more happiness and balance in your life as you "clean up" the energies around you. Feel free to adapt the Protocol to your own traditions.

This Protocol is a template that you can adapt to every situation by substituting a few words. When you go through it the first time at the start of a session, your intention is to prepare yourself for accurate dowsing (Steps 1 – 6).

In Step 6, focus on the specific issue you are addressing. For example, you could dowse for where the best place is for a driller to drill to obtain a sustainable source of good tasting water that meets all regulatory requirements and is sufficient to meet the needs of the client. Adapt Step 6 to the specific client you are dowsing for including their specific requirements.

Allow the pendulum to swing freely as you go through the Protocol, and ask it to indicate YES to show you that the steps are complete. If you get a NO response at any stage, you know you need to resolve that step before going on. For stubborn issues, use "Create an energy matrix" (Step 8) to reduce non-beneficial barriers and increase beneficial influences over time.

ALWAYS use a good dowsing protocol before you dowse. Use the first 5 steps of this Protocol to get YOURSELF ready to dowse. Then check with Step 6 to see if it is right for you to dowse on a particular topic now. Adapt this Protocol to your needs by changing or adding any other words or prayers that feel right.

*(For a more detailed explanation of the Dowsing Protocol, tools and dowsing, please refer to my other books, listed near the front: **Dowsing That Works - Use a Protocol to Get Results** and **Bridge Matter and Spirit with Dowsing** available from www.dowser.ca and Amazon.)*

The Dowsing Protocol summary

1. Balance your physical body

Find a quiet time and focus your intention to bring yourself into a calm, balanced sate of mind and body.

2. Connect to the Dowsing System

With dowsing tool in hand (to confirm responses) say: *"For the best and highest good of All Creation* (or however you address the Divine Source), *I ask*:

- *to be connected to my human body for my good health*
- *to be connected with the intelligent/beneficial energies of nature*
- *to be connected and in resonance with Divine Good*
- *to be connected, guided and protected by my Spirit Team*
- *for the assistance of beneficial energies*
- *that my dowsing be 100% accurate*

    Check the tool's signals for YES, NO, DISCONNECT and MAXIMIZE.

    Set your INTENTION: what do you want to accomplish in the session? Ask for the assistance of beneficial energies in resonance with you and the **Divine Source** who have useful information to share at this time to assist you in achieving your Intention. Check for the presence of these beneficial energies. Confirm that they are aligned with the Best and Highest Good.

3. Forgive yourself

We cannot be accurate if we have not forgiven ourselves and those around us. Say: *"Creator, forgive me. I forgive myself. I forgive all those who have harmed me. I release them from my body mind and spirit."* If you cannot forgive someone, at least give them back the accountability for their actions.

4. Clear yourself of nonbeneficial energies

Say: *"For the best and highest good of all creation and as appropriate, I ask that the frequency of all nonbeneficial energies (emotions, thought forms, attachments etc.) and processes associated with every aspect of my being (physical, mental, spiritual, emotional, and energetic) be immediately removed in all dimensions, time frames, realities, and frequencies, and that the energies be transformed for the best and highest good of all creation and as appropriate.* (Repeat for as long as your dowsing tool shows disconnecting motion. If the tool doesn't stop after three repeats, proceed to Step 8.)

5. Maximize your energy field

Say: "I ask

- *that my energy field be maximized for the best and highest good of All Creation and as appropriate*
- *that all aspects of my physical, mental, spiritual, emotional and energetic being exist in perfect health in all dimensions, time frames, frequencies and realities.* (Repeat for as long as your dowsing tool shows maximizing motion. If the tool doesn't stop after three repeats, proceed to Step 8)

6. Seek permission to dowse

If you get a NO to any of the following questions, do not proceed:

- *"May I dowse for _______?* (Permission)
- *Can I dowse for _______?* (Ability)
- *Should I dowse for _____?"* (Karmic path)

7. Dowse

Use the processes described in steps 4 and 5 above, and apply them to the situation for which you are dowsing. Dowsing works best when you're in a state of ignorance and apathy: you don't know the answer, and you don't care what it is.

Tips: Keep the question clear and literal, assume nothing, use a chart for accuracy, respect others' privacy, don't dowse unless requested to by the person the service is for, dowse in service for others not for personal greed, never diagnose or offer medical advice unless you are a licensed medical practitioner.

8. Create a matrix if needed (automatic energy system)

If the situation doesn't resolve itself within a few minutes, ask that an ever-changing energy matrix be established in the appropriate place, staffed by the appropriate Beings that will automatically adjust and transform all nonbeneficial energies as needed to fulfill the intention.

9. Disconnect

Once the session is complete, fully, consciously, actively and as appropriate at this time, disconnect from all energies with which you have been interacting. (You may stay connected to the Divine Source and your Spirit Team and other energies that continue to assist you.) Use the dowsing tool, or you can simply clap your hands with intent to accomplish this important step. Some energies may stay active if you have set up a matrix in Step 8.

10. Thank
Thank all energies that have assisted you.

11. Communicate your results appropriately
If you are dowsing for someone else, be sure to check what results can be communicated to the subject for the best and highest good of all creation. Never discuss anything with anyone in a way that could identify the subject. Be discreet.

Troubleshooting

What if your pendulum doesn't work?

I received a letter from a new dowser who was discouraged because her pendulum just kept indicating "NO" whenever she asked it any question. She wrote: *"My dowsing isn't going well. I don't know if it's because I'm not focused enough. I'm starting to get very discouraged and think maybe I should stop trying dowsing when I'm not up to par, but that would defeat the whole purpose [of dowsing]. I'm discouraged and waiting for your comments."*

I think all dowsers have experienced times when the pendulum won't seem to co-operate with us. When I've had consistent NOs from the pendulum, I've learned that often there's something I have to work out for myself or it's just not the right time for me to dowse.

Here are some questions I ask when I'm not getting the answers I expect:

Is there something I need to do first?
For example: eat, drink water, go to the bathroom, go to work, meditate, sleep, clean the house, take my medication, talk to someone, clear an earth energy, go outside and breathe, go to my doctor, look after my kids, make a phone call, use my normal conscious skills to achieve something, etc.

Should I be using a different tool?
For example: L rods, different pendulum, my body, review information in a book

Should I dowse in a different place/time of day?

Sometimes the furnace, fridge or other electrical devices in the proximity can set up interference or we're just too tired to be accurate.

Should I ask to communicate with a different Guide?
It's surprising how often this is the case - you may need to bring in a "specialist" Being to assist you. Ask for the assistance of a Beneficial Being in resonance with you and "Divine Source" who has useful information to share at this time.

Should I be using my dowsing in service for others instead of for myself?
I find my best accuracy comes from spending time in service for someone else.

Should I be asking a different question or focusing on a different area?
Maybe it's just not the right time to focus on what you're asking.

Is a Nonbeneficial Being or energy interfering with my dowsing?
Depending on the type of dowsing I'm doing, I may get interference. If this happens I use the Dowsing Protocol to get back to strengthen my accuracy.

Don't be discouraged at getting NO's while you're dowsing. It can be a sign that you have some work to do. Challenges force you to grow. I've found that if one doesn't step up to meet and overcome challenges, then dowsing system may not work so well. Our Guides are very keen for us to learn, and one way to make us learn more is to make the pendulum "stop working". When this happens, think of itas an opportunity to take another step on your path.

**Remember to use a Dowsing Protocol
every time before you dowse!**

Practice
The way to become a good dowser is to practice until using the Dowsing Protocol and a pendulum seem like second nature. The first day you learn to dowse is probably not the best day to dowse questions about Aliens! When you are emotional while dowsing, or become emotional when you get a dowsing response, your accuracy will not be as good as if you are calm before, during and after a session.

If you are fearful of the answers you might get, or don't take what you're doing seriously, then the answers you get through dowsing will be meaningless at best, and dangerous at worst. How can dowsing be dangerous? If you take action on the wrong information, you will very likely be making bad decision.

One of the things I use dowsing for is to always find good parking spots. Other people use it to find lost golf balls. Find something neutral to practice with.

Following, is a list of dowsing questions to practice on. They may be boring, but they shouldn't trigger an emotional response. If they do, choose different questions! Remember that dowsing works best from a place of ignorance and apathy: you don't know the answer, and you don't care what it is.

Unless you are already an experienced dowser, or know someone who is who can help you, I'd suggest a week of practice on neutral subjects before you start the questions on Aliens and Alien interaction in the sections that follow.

Survey 1: Practice dowsing questions

	Y	N	Practice questions
1			Do I have a valid driver's license?
2			Have I drunk some coffee today?
3			Can I hear a bird singing right now?
4			Can I see the sky from where I am sitting?
5			Can I smell flowers right now?
6			Do I have shoes on my feet right now?
7			Is my dowsing accurate? LOW MEDIUM HIGH

5 Create Psychic Protection

"I must not fear. Fear is the mind-killer. I will face my fear. I will permit it to pass over me and through me. And when it has gone past I will turn the inner eye to see its path. Where the fear has gone there will be nothing. Only I will remain."
Frank Herbert, Dune Chronicles

I had nightmares for most of my life. Some were the usual anxiety-based dreams, such as missing airplanes or being naked in public and some were full on visions of demons with gaping jaws coming after me.

As a child I dreamt I was climbing attic stairs to open the door to black, faceless creatures I knew were on the other side of it. I'm not sure if I meant to let them out or go in with them, but they were the same ones that I would see hovering over my bed, and that I propelled myself awake from. In my dream I thought it was silly that other people were afraid of these black creatures. I felt that way until the moment my hand rested on the doorknob and I was suddenly overwhelmed with horror by what I was about to do. I was pretty sure the creatures on the other side of the door knew I was there and I was afraid of what they might do to me. Fortunately, I seem to have the gift of waking up, so that's what I did.

Being clairsentient and being aware of things around me I couldn't see even while I was awake, I stayed in a state of fear until I was about 46 years old. I thought the world was full of ghosts and they were all out to get me. To be honest, it never occurred to me to be afraid of Alien Beings.

(I was also diagnosed with rheumatoid arthritis at 29 and developed other immune disorders that I took a variety of drugs to control, but that's another story.)

In 1999 I found dowsing (see Dowsing Fundamentals, page 29) and learned to be comfortable with the unseen world around me and over time, be able to safely interact with it. The most important thing I learned while I was moving from fearful to fearless, was the importance of having psychic protection BEFORE interacting with the energy world. It's far easier to prevent a problem than to fix it after it's rooted.

I found other energy modalities as well, and began to use all of them to get over my fears of my experiences. It is important to be able to quickly discern which energies are beneficial to us and which are not. Be prepared, and be safe. Later in this chapter we will look at techniques for removing Nonbeneficial energy

Techniques to manage Alien interaction*

We are the birthright beings of Earth and must exercise free will, choosing to be sovereign over our own beings. In some of my dealings with some Alien consciousness I have noticed that they seem to have a "hive mind" and do not care to interact with people who question their authority.

Humans by our nature are disruptive. You can demonstrate your independence by training yourself to retain your power through the exercise of conscious will. Your strength is within you. If you feel in danger, stay calm, come to whatever level of alertness you can manage, and ask for the assistance of Beneficial Beings in resonance with you and the "Divine Source" (or however you refer to your highest spiritual principle) who can help you now.

Learn to tame your emotions by practicing objective compassion during your waking hours. If you can release fear and judgment, you will be able to remain in control of your body in all circumstances.

Whether you want to completely eliminate any contact with Alien Beings, or develop the ability to safely interact with them, you need to do something to manage the process.

Stay in control

The main thing to do in any interaction with Alien or other interdimensional Beings is to stay in control of your own emotions and thoughts. As in the rest of our lives, all we can really do, aside from taking the appropriate safety precautions, is to control our reactions to what is going on around us. Thinking clearly helps us retain control over our state of consciousness, so that we can bring ourselves to our full power at will and with the ability to break the contact if you feel uncomfortable or have any sense of danger.

All stories of Alien abduction that I am aware of have occurred when the person is an altered state of consciousness. Perhaps abduction can only occur in this state, so it stands to reason that if we can retain our full range of consciousness, nothing will occur without our consent.

Alien consciousness may adapt these techniques to remove themselves from their Human hosts and return to their proper state and place of being.

For myself, through my dowsing, I am definitely aware of other beings in my vicinity, and I control the interactions by both opening and closing the channels at my discretion. If I feel Beings trying to get my attention, I am able to defer contact to a later time that is convenient for me. Anyone can learn to do this.

Box 2: A child's ghost story

> **A child's ghost story**
>
> A related example of this is a story about a young child who was convinced that there were "ghosts" in his bedroom. It was upsetting to him to say the least, and he complained about it to his parents from the time he could talk until he was six years old. The experiences finally stopped when he was told him that if there were ghosts in his room, they were simply jealous of him and all he had to do was tell them to go away. He did and they did.
>
> There are a couple of lessons here: if a child or adult tells you they are experiencing something unusual, take it seriously and ask them to tell you more about it, then help them to deal with the situation. Another lesson, is that even a determined child can stop interference from other-dimensional beings if they believe they have the power to do so.

A way of staying in your power is by always using the Dowsing Protocol (page 31) to manage inter-dimensional communications. Step 2 builds an energy shield between you and the unknown. Step 8 makes the shield permanent, so you should never find yourself in a vulnerable position. If you do feel threatened, reactivate your Protocol. If you continue to feel threatened, terminate the connection.

Don't allow Alien Beings to name themselves

When encountering Alien beings, don't ask them their names or where they come from. Allowing them to name themselves may give them power over you because, as mentioned earlier, their telepathic abilities will enable them to choose a name from your world view that either inspires awe or terror and may not reveal anything about their true nature or origin.

When I encounter unknown energies, I simply dowse how many there are and assign them numbers. Then I dowse which numbered being to communicate with. Interestingly, in some situations, there may be several beings present, but they are not aware of each other. (This is true both with ghost busting and Alien busting.) I find their lack of awareness somewhat surprising, but it does support the view that these energies exist in different dimensions and are not fully present in ours, unless we allow them to manifest.

Get help from Beneficial Beings

It can be very hard to tell Beneficial from Nonbeneficial Beings, but if we do find some that are in resonance with you and the "Divine Source" and who accept Divine Holy Love, then it is possible to learn things and get useful information from them on a variety of topics.

I personally believe I have benefited through resonating with Alien and other forms of consciousness. How do you get to that point? Through finding the place in yourself that is love. Get there by remembering the feeling of love of nature or of your family or of your pet. Remember a time when you felt and experienced love.

If you can go into that place in yourself, you will conquer all the fear there is, and you will teach by being – you will heal yourself, those around you and even the Aliens.

The Dowsing Protocol

Dowsing and The Dowsing Protocol are discussed at length in Dowsing Fundamentals (page 29). For me and for many people, it has proven to be effective time and again as a way of understanding and bringing balance to a wide variety of situations. If you want to get technical as to how it works, I believe that dowsing is the collapse of the quantum wave of possibilities through our intention and physical action. But you don't need to understand how it works for dowsing to be effective, just learn the techniques and practice them.

Focus on Step 4 of the Dowsing Protocol (page 31) to remove all aspects of Alien interference. Then move to Step 5 to create and maximize healthy human energy patterns. Step 8 will help you maintain beneficial energies in all aspects of your being.

Once you have re-established your sovereign being you may choose to initiate healthy, safe contact between yourself and Alien energy. (See **Initiating Contact with Alien Beings** page 75.)

Step 4 of the Dowsing Protocol: Disconnect Alien interference

Alien energies may be attracted to a place or person by activities and thoughts (such as with groups that meet to discuss UFOs.) With dowsing you can remove these energies and restore balance using Step 4 of the Protocol. It is best to ask for the assistance of *"Beneficial energy beings in resonance with yourself and the Divine Source that can assist at this time in providing information and energies to remove all energies that do not assist you or the birthright beings of the Earth."* I know this seems like a lot of words, but I've always found that being specific about what you want and don't want helps achieve the desired results.

Do this with as much love and compassion (for all Beings) that you can manage. Tell them that you don't have what that they want or need, and that you won't help them or cooperate with them in any way. Stay conscious, be sovereign in your own Being and tell them to leave. An attitude of fear, judgement or anger will not get rid of them, and will likely just make them stronger. For you own long-term safety, do not try to personally fight or command them, simply ask the Divine Source to manage the situation. You are simply the facilitator. Do not engage.

A. Do the Dowsing Protocol Steps 1 – 6. (Page 31)

B. State your intention (such as): *"to prevent any, or any further interactions with Alien Beings which I do not approve of or initiate."*

C. Swinging the pendulum say: *"I ask the Divine Source to immediately remove the frequencies of all non-beneficial energies (emotions, thought forms, attachments etc.) associated with every aspect of Alien contact (including physical, mental, spiritual, emotional, and energetic aspects) from every aspect of my being in all dimensions, all time frames, all realities, and all frequencies."*

Repeat this statement until the pendulum stops. If it doesn't stop, after repeating the statement three times, go to Step 8 of the Dowsing Protocol to set up an automatic process.

D. Dowse: *"Is Alien interference still active in my energy field?"* If YES, repeat C, above. Repeat until you bring interference from Alien energy to neutral. Let the dowsing guide you – don't try to force the process. Fundamental change can take some time to integrate, so always ask for results to be experienced at the appropriate rate. You may have to do this over a period of several days. You can put in an automatic program to maintain good balance using Step 8 of the Protocol, below.

Step 5 of the Dowsing Protocol: Create and maximize health

Once you have disconnected any Alien interference you can activate healthy energies in your life to replace any stress the former situation may have created.

Set your intention to experience well-being and abundance in your physical, mental, emotional, spiritual and energetic beings, and in all aspects of your personal and professional relationships and endeavours. This section can also help with Soul repair and retrieval in case any parts of your original Soul have splintered off through Alien (or other) interaction.

Remember that since we're human, there will always be times when things don't seem perfect, but don't lapse into fear or judgement. Rely on the Dowsing Protocol (and your common sense!) to keep you safe using the steps below.

1. Do the Dowsing Protocol, Steps 1- 6.

2. Set your intention (such as): *"I want to be a safe, healthy, fully human being in control of my life."*

3. Use Step 5 of the Dowsing Protocol: Swinging the pendulum say *"As appropriate I ask the Divine Source to maximize my energy field for the best and highest good of all creation, particularly for me, so that I am a safe, fully human being in control of my experiences. I ask that all aspects of my physical, mental, spiritual, emotional and energetic being exist in perfect human health in all dimensions, time frames, frequencies and realities. I ask that all aspects of my Soul and Self meant to be in this body, according to my birthright, be repaired and returned and fully and easily integrated into all aspects of my sovereign human being"* (Repeat for as long as your dowsing tool shows maximizing motion.

4. If the pendulum l doesn't stop after three times, proceed to Step 8 of the Dowsing Protocol to create lasting psychic protection that will continually create the conditions for you to be a safe, healthy, fully human being. For example: *"I ask that an ever-changing, Divine energy matrix be established in the appropriate place that will automatically adjust and transform all non-beneficial Alien energies as needed to fulfill my intentions to be a fully, sovereign human being."*

Affirmations

Saying affirmations is a well-known way of training the brain to create resonant frequencies that can attract things that you want. It is a form of magic and is also referred to as the Law of Attraction. You can use affirmations with dowsing to create even stronger results.

Say the following statements (and others of your own devising) out loud while swinging your pendulum. The vibration of the spoken words plus the movement of the pendulum can help to create the results more strongly. A YES response will confirm if they are true for you at this time, a NO response shows you where you need to some work. If the pendulum gives you a NO response to any of these statements, then you know where you have work to do and you can use the Dowsing Protocol (page 31) to disconnect barriers to your experience of being in a healthy state of being.

As a physical reminder, you can also draw a picture of yourself, put a circle around it, and fill it up with the beneficial energy generated by the following statements.

Before you begin the affirmations, be clear in your own mind what you are trying to do: it could be to prevent Alien influence, remove Alien influence or for the brave: create Alien interaction! Be careful what you wish for, and please take the work seriously.

You'll notice the last affirmation is with regard to serving others. I've always found the best results for me come as a result of serving others.

1. I am safe and protected because I am in resonance with the Divine Source.

2. All my actions, thoughts, words and intuitions are guided by the Divine Source for the best and highest good of all creation and the birthright beings of Earth.

3. I am always in the right place at the right time.

4. I am as aware of the energies around me as I need to be and when I choose to be.

5. I am strong and healthy in all aspects of my being.

6. I always think clearly.

7. I seek the truth.

8. The Divine Source works through me.

9. I am grateful for my abilities, and use them responsibly to serve others.

Emotional Freedom Technique

Another way of creating psychic protection and removing unwanted energies is Emotional Freedom Technique. EFT (sometimes called "Tapping") is well established as a way of overcoming Post Traumatic Stress Disorder (PTSD) and other emotional issues. It works by encouraging the body systems not to shut down when confronted by an emotional memory by self-tapping different parts of the body and repeating simple statements.

Founder Gary Craig's website (www.emofree.com) offers a lot of free information and I encourage you to browse his information to learn the proper techniques. Once you've done that, you can dowse to see if it will be beneficial to you to use some of the following statements with EFT in order to create psychic protection.

EFT Statements

1. Even though I sometimes feel like I have had bad experiences with Alien interactions, I deeply love and respect myself.

2. Even though I am sometimes afraid of going to sleep because I'm afraid I won't be safe, I deeply love and accept myself.

3. Even though it sometimes seems like things are out to get me, I deeply love and respect myself.

4. Even though I sometimes worry that Aliens have done something to me that I can't remember, I deeply love and accept myself.

5. Even though I sometimes worry that Aliens have put something in my body that I don't want, I deeply love and respect myself.

6. Even though I sometimes think that I come from another planet, I deeply love and accept myself.

7. Even though I often feel that I don't belong on Earth, I deeply love and respect myself.

8. Even though there are many things I am afraid of and don't understand, I deeply love and accept myself.

Reprogram the Experience

Once you have your emotions under control, you can do things to neutralize traumatic memories and mental triggers of something that happened. You can also to prepare yourself for anticipated trauma.

This is the kind of thing that people who drive long distances train themselves to do in case either an animal jumps into the path of their vehicle or another vehicle stops suddenly in front of them. The driver will choose either to swerve and avoid the obstruction or to keep going in a straight line, depending on the size of the obstruction, the surrounding traffic and the road conditions. Drivers prepare themselves for the unexpected so that their physical systems respond automatically in a crisis.

You can do this as well to reprogram any traumatic memories associated with any nonbeneficial Alien (or Human) interaction. Even if you don't believe you are strong enough, act as if you are and you will both get results and become stronger. Try the thought experiment below.

Box 3: Thought Experiment One: Change the memory

Thought Experiment One: Change the memory
Remember what happened.
What do you wish had happened?
What would you say?
What would do differently?
Replay the memory as you wish it had happened.

The Dream Time

Before you go to sleep at night, set your intention to remember your dreams and to receive information that will be useful to you. Add the strong intention that you will wake up if you are "in trouble" or are having a nightmare in your dream. When you wake up, remember the situation, imagine a better solution to an issue you may have uncovered, then go back to sleep, and dream the new scenario.

When you wake up, jot down what you remember, and think about what it might mean. With practice, your dreams will become more meaningful and this will help resolve issues both in the dreamtime and in your normal waking state. Work with reprogramming your dreams.

It is possible to wake up from a bad dream, think of a better outcome for the dream, then go back to sleep and create a new outcome.

Perhaps we experience Déjà vu experiences in the dream time. (See page 16 for discussion).

Ceremony

You can create psychic protection using ceremony either as part of a community or on your own. Go through each room in ceremony with the intention of bringing balance. Have windows open so that energies can disperse more easily. You may use sounds, such as a bell, drum or chime, or simply your voice or hand claps to help break up stagnant energy.

Create a ceremony that consists of the following elements:

1. Release the past and all beings, thoughts, energies, emotions, memories etc. that are no longer needed.

2. State what you want in your life (health, prosperity, love, etc.)
3. Ask for the Divine Source to manifest what is appropriate.

4. Place objects in dowsed locations to anchor the ceremony.

Find Community

Finding like-minded people to talk to is a very powerful way to feel safe. When you feel like you're the only one going through something, it can be frightening. When you know there are others you can discuss issues with, it can be reassuring. Not all of us are blessed with family members or friends we can share these experiences with, so find a group, either on-line or in person and be part of a community. There is strength in numbers.

Physical protection versus energy remedies

Physical objects, coupled with a strong intention to create protection, can help anchor your psychic protection by helping you focus on what you want. When you generate frequencies that are resonant with the Divine Source, frequencies that do not hold the same resonance cannot enter your space. If you live in fear, then fear resonance will bring fearful beings to you. When you live in a state of love or compassion, you will attract compassionate, Beneficial Beings to you. You may need to practice to control your fear. Have courage – if you don't have it, act like you do until you do.

　　　　　　　　　　　　　　

Get yourself an object that you can keep on your body or place around your house or property to remind you that you are strong. Power objects can include personal religious pictures or items, rings or jewelry, photographs, items of clothing or objects that contain sacred geometry designs, crystals or other things that remind you of your strength. Smudging, the practice of allowing the smoke from smouldering sage or other forms of incense, to pass across the body and through rooms can provide energy balancing plus a sensory reminder of psychic protection.

Give the problem form, then destroy it

The basic formula for transforming non-beneficial energy is to give it form and then destroy it. The physical remedies help give the problem form. When we destroy or alter the form, the problem is destroyed.

If you have some visual impression of the intrusive Beings that you don't want around you, see them shrink into a point of light and disappear. Or you can make a drawing representing the Alien energy, then rip it up and burn it. Give them form, then destroy them. If you have begun the session with the Dowsing Protocol, you will always be safe and never be given more than you can handle.

6 Dowse about Alien Beings

*"[God] created beings and he let them develop
according to the internal laws with which He endowed
each one ... He gave autonomy to the beings of the
universe ... giving life to every reality."*

Pope Francis
Casina of Pius IV, October 27, 2014

A brief history of Alien Beings

The word "alien" is simply an adjective that refers to someone or something that is not from a geographic area. In modern usage, it has come to be used as a noun and generally refers to extraterrestrial (ET) (from the Latin *"outside of earth"*) life forms, or people trying to cross national borders illegally. It seems to me that referring to a someone as an "Alien" is somewhat pejorative. Yes, the person in question may not be from this area, and may be fleeing conditions in their homelands, but these labels tend to rob individuals of their humanity.

Can an "Alien" – a being originating from outside of Earth - have humanity? That's a question of semantics. Would we say, assuming they exist, that they possess *"alienity"* just as we have *"humanity"*? And what about *"inalienable rights"* (rights that cannot be taken away from the possessor of them)? How did the word *"alien"* get into the middle of that?

Clearly we can get a bit tongue-tied in this discussion of what to call visitors from off-planet, so for simplicity's sake, in this book, I will primarily refer to Aliens as *"Alien Beings"*, and I may refer to them with other adjectives such as *"Beneficial Beings"*. Other books may seek to classify Alien Beings by species. In this book we will classify them by characteristics.

The current head of the Catholic Church, Pope Francis, surprised many people when he referred to the *"beings of the universe"* (see quote at the top of this page) and inferred that there might be more than one *"reality"*. The Dalai Lama, winner of the Nobel Peace Prize in 1989 and the spiritual leader of Tibetan Buddhism, has suggested that if another sentient being comes from a distant galaxy that we should try to shake their hands if they have one! These two religious and world leaders have a refreshingly natural attitude.

Popular culture has given us a hodgepodge of images to choose from. From lovable ones such as *"My Favourite Martian"*, *"E.T."*, *"Alf"*, and *"Yoda"* to creepy ones such as the menacing creatures that appeared in the movies *"Men in Black"*, the *"Alien"* series and many others.

The idea of Aliens or *"gods from above"* has always appealed to human story tellers. In a typical narrative, a star being of some kind descends to earth and interacts with and often tests humans to see if they are of good character. Star Beings can be hard to recognize because they often take an unattractive form when they come to Earth. In the stories, only true love can recognize them, and when that occurs, the Star Being is revealed in his or her glory and the human may have an opportunity to visit the star world.

The stories are generally based around the visible constellations and stars such as the Pleiades, the Big Dipper and Sirius, but sometimes just refer to the Sky People. Here is an Algonquin (native North American) story about the Star People with a slightly different plot twist and message.

Box 4: Algon and the Sky Girl

Algon and the Sky Girl (Algonquin – abbreviated)
"Algon found a strange circle cut in the prarie grass. Hiding, he saw a willow basket descend from the sky bearing twelve beautiful maidens." Algon devised a plana to kidnap the youngest and most beautiful of them. *"He took her to his village and in time she fell in love with him. They had a son and lived happily for a time.*

"As the years passed the Sky-Girl grew homesick so she built a magic willow basket and headed for her family in the sky. Every day Algon went to sit in the magic circle hoping she would return."

Eventually the Sky-Girl's father brings Algon to the sky to meet the Sky-People and said *"they should always be free to travel between the sky-country and the Earth and so their descendants became falcons and still fly high and swoop down over the forests and prairies.*

What is overwhelming in these shared stories, is their consistency across many cultures and many time periods. They seem to point to a history of Human interaction with Alien Beings.

The evidence

The stories, coupled with astounding archaeological evidence (such as *"Puma Punku"* in Bolivia) and various paintings (such as *"The Madonna with Saint Giovannino"* by Domenico Ghirlandaio) are not easily explained by conventional history. Don Donderi, former Associate Dean of the Faculty of Graduate Studies and Research at Magill University in Canada, has compiled an impressive catalogue of evidence.in his book *"UFOs, ETs and Alien Abductions."*

How do Aliens get here?

From the Our Universe chapter (page 23) we can safely say that humans currently don't understand how Alien Beings show up on Earth. I believe travel is inter-dimensional. It may be by folding Space-time through the manipulation of Black Holes, or Wormholes or be reducing their forms to electromagnetic energy that can travel faster than light then rematerialize in our earth dimension. It may also be that the Beings we call Aliens are already here and living simultaneously with us curled up in the dimensions described by String Theory and/or in all that space between the atoms. Or in the mysterious Dark matter and energy (page 25) that we know so little about.

I suggest that for Alien Beings to manifest in our dimensional awareness, they need to dock onto resonant frequencies here on Earth. These frequencies become a portal or doorway that they can enter through.

Portals

Portals are places where Alien energy can manifest in our dimension. These doorways may occur naturally in places of fluctuating electromagnetic energy or may be created by Humans with intention and ceremony.

Creating places for Divine energy to show up has always been the focus of both occult and mainstream philosophical, religious practice. This is why we have built churches and created other types of sacred space such as personal altars: so that we may feel the presence of the Divine Source. Officiants seek to create a resonant environment where the Beings they seek can manifest. A congregation of seekers repeats ritualistic phrases, postures and actions to attract what they seek. Once a certain frequency is attained, it is possible to attract a being of another frequency. (See Ceremony, page 48.)

I suggest that Alien energy may be able to dock on Earth in places wherever there are thought forms and emotions relating to them – either thoughts of yearning for them or fear of them. When they do show up, they may take the form they are expected to because they seem to have telepathic abilities.

What do Aliens look like?

The current UFO literature catalogues a variety of Alien types ranging from the *"Reptilians"* (it's easy to imagine them) to the *"Greys"* (the little guys with big eyes and no clothes) and the *"Tall Whites"* (also easy to imagine.)

While these species may exist, my personal theory is that all extraterrestrial life visiting Earth is essentially electromagnetic in nature and takes form once it gets here. What form does it take once it's here? The one we expect it to. I believe there is a telepathic component to their appearance and they are able to adapt their appearances to our expectations. So if you expect to see certain physical characteristics, such as green, scaly skin, you will.   One of the reasons I've come to this conclusion is from my experience photographing Orbs. Whatever they are, they have the ability to both interact with the observer and change form.

Orb shape shifters

The presence of "Orbs" (the fluffy, circular shapes that show up in many photographs) has lead people to ask if they are evidence of Spirit or Alien presence. Some people dismiss the images as simply dust particles or digital artifacts, but I believe that the images may represent unknown aspects of the multi-dimensionality of our universe, including Alien and other forms of consciousness (including our own!).

Orbs are often photographed around cemeteries, churches, monuments and gathering places. These sites have their own built-in sacred space, developed over the years by peoples' natural reverence or emotional context.

I have taken thousands of pictures of Orbs since 2005 (Details in my book *"Meeting Orbs in Sacred Space".*) I know they are conscious and that they can enter and leave our awareness at times of their own choosing and yet they can be coaxed in by some people.

With dowsing it may be possible to communicate with these phenomena, or to at least to understand what triggers their presence.

Orbs can show up with different colours and structures based on the individual's personal physical, mental, spiritual, cultural and emotional energies as well as the person's brain wave resonance. (See **Consciousness and perception** page 14.) Orbs can "shape shift", from circular orbs to plasma/mist and then into other forms. I have seen Orb energy transition into something approaching human form. Orbs can move in response to our behaviours and thought forms.

Perhaps Aliens enter our dimension as orb energies, then transition into a form that we expect to see. Once locked into a form, it may be difficult to distinguish between them and the birthright Beings of Earth.

Below is a description of an "Alien orb" experience that an energetically sensitive person had while she slept. Why are orb energies hanging around us? Perhaps they have a purpose – perhaps one of the purposes is to heal humans. Following is an example of one such story sent to me by a colleague.

Box 5: Alien Orbs

> *"Alien orbs healing me while I slept*
> M. recorded me on her iPhone while I was falling asleep [for an unrelated medical reason]. *The orbs showed up everywhere: above me, between me and the bottom of the door and in the background. The carpet is distorted as if there is a stronger energy present. I did nothing to make it happen.*
>
> *I thought that they were spirits doing something, but a trusted medium said that they were Greys* [Aliens] *and that they were doing repair work on my kidneys and liver. Once I became aware of their work, I "turned on" that portion of my senses to allow me to feel their presence.*
>
> *We routinely have beings of all sorts in our bedroom, and are no longer bothered by them. It seems to be much easier to communicate with them when we are sleeping. Lee Ann P"*.

The uncanny valley

The tech industry uses the phrase *"uncanny valley"* to refer to an artificial humanoid figure closely resembling a human, but which arouses a sense of unease in the viewer. If an Alien Being (or machine) is trying to shape shift to conform to a mental image of what you expect to see, but can't quite lock on to you, the Being may randomly choose an image that closely resembles someone you know (perhaps someone deceased) and then take that form in order to keep you relaxed during interactions. (Of course, if you see the form resembling a deceased relative, it may actually be the residual energy of that loved on, so don't assume everything is an Alien!)

I have personally heard from an Abductee that on several occasions he felt he had been placed into a completely artificial visual environment that he felt was meant to be reassuring to him. The problem (for the Aliens) was that he was able to maintain enough conscious awareness to realize that the environment was fake because certain small details weren't quite right. The Abductee was in the "uncanny valley".

Dowsing with discernment can help provide answers if you question whether the people and experiences you are having are authentically human. Simply dowse: *"Is this person 100% human?"* If you get a "NO" response, be careful. You can sometimes recognize imposters by where they are and how they're dressed. If they're not dressed for the climate (for example, in sandals and shorts in deep snow or walking along a deserted road with no car or house in sight, you may be looking at a Being that is not fully human. They may have taken an inappropriate form, then been stuck with it

Whether it is an Alien, a ghost or something else is up to you to figure out with dowsing.

Do Aliens speak English?

Not all things speak English, of course, but once you have established a relationship with your Guides (Step 2 on the Dowsing Protocol, page 31), you can use them as universal translators. It is important to communicate only through your Guides, never directly. They are your buffer to the other realms, and if you work properly through them, you will always be safe and protected while you're working out there on the fringes of rational thought.

In my early days of communicating with other-dimensional beings I would sometimes get confusing words from them. At one point they were transmitting a new language to me that they wanted to use as a basis of communication. They would also sometimes communicate in Latin and I would have to look up the meaning of things.

I decided that in order for me to work efficiently in the time I had available, I needed to communicate in English, so I asked the Beings to communicate clearly in ways I could understand. This has worked very well for me, and someday when I have time I will take steps to communicate with them in a way of their choosing. The point is this: you can take steps to control the flow of information and Beneficial Beings will cooperate. Other ways that Aliens might attempt communication are through signs such as objects going missing and then reappearing, symbols, telepathic thought, direct contact, visions, dreams and dowsing.

Always use psychic protection (Chapter 5) before attempting any type of communication. I have seen some highly sensitive people lose their connection to our standard reality by roaming too far into the other realms without being careful and having adequate protection (such as using a Dowsing Protocol), It can be seductive to be "out there", and sometimes people don't want to come back to our standard Earth reality. Some don't even know they've gone. Never treat this work lightly.

Why don't more Alien Beings contact Humans?

Off-planet Beings may be interacting with Humans on a regular basis, however they may be doing so in such a way that we don't know about it. They may cloak their activities so as not frighten us. (See Alien Orbs page 55). Not many people are ready to handle the strangeness of a "space ship" landing in their front yards, but most people will appreciate help from a stranger who suddenly appears to help them, or who they meet casually yet have an unusually intense conversation that helps them with their life path. People can more easily accept that an Angel helped them than an Alien.

One of the questions I ask with my dowsing tools when encountering an apparently human individual who appears unexpectedly, is to ask if they are fully human. I sometimes get a NO. I then ask if these beings are Beneficial or Nonbeneficial to me. If they are Beneficial I ask them if they have a communication for me, if not, I do not engage with them unless my Guides indicate I should help them get to where they need to be. I often encounter beings that would like to get back home and don't know how. I help them home.

We will talk discuss this further in Chapter 9, **Initiating Contact** (page 75).

Why do Alien Beings want to come to Earth?

I think there are different motivations to visit Earth, just as humans have different reasons to visit other countries: some to do academic research, some to go sightseeing and eat different foods, some to help places recover from natural disasters, some for medical tourism and some for sexual tourism. The same is very likely true for Alien Beings, there is no "one size fits all" reason.

I think honestly that in the Alien realms, Earth is the party planet. We have sensation here – we have emotion. We have food and drink and so many sensory opportunities. This is also the planet of pain – with sensory experience and choice we often experience pain, physically, mentally, emotionally, spiritually and energetically. As humans it is our job to learn to cope with pain and to learn not inflict it on others. These can be hard lessons, and even Alien Beings don't necessarily want to have to learn them. Their problem is they don't know about the pain side of the equation until they get here.

I believe there are Beneficial Beings who can interact with us in ways that we are not usually aware of. With training, we can be aware of them when we choose to be. The Dream time can be a powerful opportunity for connection with beings. (See page 21.)

Spirit Guides, Walk-Ins, Star Children (etc.)

Whether you call them Spirit Guides, Angels, Beings of Light, **Ascended Masters**, Aliens, **Walk-Ins**, **Star Children** or *whatever*, I believe there are non-visible beings co-existing in our own and other dimensions.

Some people believe that they themselves have off-planet origins. According to the generally accepted Big Bang theory, everything that is now, was tightly packed together at the moment of expansion. In that regard, everything in our universe is all made of the same stuff, so it's easy to see that we might consider ourselves made of the same stuff as the stars and other Universal Beings.

Brad Steiger, in his 1982 book *"Star People"* defined Star Children this way: *"Some human's souls came from origins beyond physical Earth and experience simultaneously in many realities, timelines, and realms."* I have met many people, including very young children, who share that odd feeling that they come from somewhere else and have a special purpose here.

Ruth Montgomery in her 1985 book *"Strangers Among Us"* defined Walk-Ins as conscious beings who had permission from host Humans to "take over" their bodies. Currently the term is more often in reference to a Being that has taken over a host body without permission.

Other forms of consciousness that we may perceive as coming from outside of ourselves include one's own "Higher Self" and "Soul".

While not everyone is gifted with sensory sensitivity, most people can learn to communicate with other-dimensional beings using dowsing tools and a focused mind.

Beneficial, Nonbeneficial and Neutral Alien Beings

Sometimes there is an offer of a gift of power that comes through interacting with Alien and other forms of interdimensional energy. We must know what kind of Being is offering this gift if we are to be safe because promises of power from Nonbeneficial Beings will gradually erode the free will of the individual. Energy gifts and information from Beneficial Beings will provide benefit to the recipients.

Beneficial Beings

Some Beings are connected to the Divine Source (the ultimate beneficial, creative energy) and are interested in supporting us for own sake and the sake of the Earth. A quick way to identify them is to ask, through dowsing, if they are in resonance with the "Divine Source" (or use the phrase reflecting your own highest spiritual principle) and if they accept "Divine Holy Love". Beings must respond "YES" to both those questions before you interact any further with them. Chapter 9, **Initiating Contact** (page 75) provides further interview questions.

Nonbeneficial Beings

Beings that are not in resonance with the Divine Source may be interested in feeding off our energy in a parasitic fashion. These Nonbeneficial Beings are attracted to people with strong energy and can trick them into thinking that the relationship will be beneficial for the human. As we progress on our spiritual path, bigger energies may be attracted to us. Nonbeneficial Beings come to check us out in order to take advantage of our energy.

Nonbeneficial Beings may promise you more power or strength or money so that you can ``do your work``, but if you don't ask where the strength comes from, you may get yourself into trouble. There may be a short term gain, but in the end you will be consumed by them. I've seen this many times with people who fall in to the trap of Ego. If you think the world is about you, you will fall. You will take on energies that ultimately do not support you.

It's easy to fall into an insidious, downward spiral where you have less and less of your own personality and free will until your energies are used up. In these cases, the human host sickens and even dies. The Nonbeneficial Alien Being doesn't care; they just go on to somebody else.

Neutral Beings

A third category of beings may be **Neutral Beings**, here to simply observe us for an unknown purpose.

Alien energies may fit into any of the above groups, and it is important to develop discernment so that you can distinguish between the ones that want to help you and the ones that want to use you for their own purposes. We need to be extremely careful before and while interacting with them. At this writing it isn't clear what percentage of Alien visitors fall into which of the above types. It's one of the questions on Survey 3: Dowse About Alien Beings. (see page 63), and I hope you will provide me with your feedback for future editions of this book.

Sometimes these Beings present themselves to you because they need help getting "home" – the place they belong, and believe you can help them do so.

Box 6: Bill and Archangel Michael at the hot tub

Bill and Archangel Michael at the hot tub

I'm reminded of Bill, a clairvoyant former colleague of mine who described being in the hot tub one evening when he saw "Archangel Michael" appear on the pool deck, flaming sword in hand. Bill took the visitation at face value and was interacting with the Being for some time before he began to feel something wasn't quite right with the energy of the Being.

He eventually realized that whatever the Being actually was, it had taken on the appearance of a figure that it had determined would be acceptable to Bill. Realizing the fraud, Bill was able to terminate the connection.

Resonance and "Divine Holy Love"

There's a phrase "Speak of the devil and it will appear". It's an old way of talking about the Law of Attraction which states that we get what we think about. If you spend your time thinking about what you don't want, that's what you will get. Think about what you want. Speak in words that reflect the life you want such as: *"I ask to be (or am grateful for being) healthy in all aspects of my being", "I ask to have experiences that create joy in my life"* or *"I ask to encounter beings that will help me develop on my human journey"*.

For your own safety, don't connect directly with new Beings, always and only communicate with Dowsing and through your Guides (Step 2 of the Dowsing Protocol). Ask the new being if they are in resonance with the "Divine Source" (or whatever your highest spiritual principle is) and if they accept "Divine Holy Love". Dowse the answer.

John Living, a well-known Canadian dowser originally from England, introduced me to the phrase *"Do you accept Divine Holy Love?"* as a tool to evaluate the safety of interacting with unknown Beings. It's not a phrase I would have used personally, but he told me then, and it's been true ever since, that if you ask that question, and the being replies "YES", then you should be safe. If it replies "NO", you should terminate the connection immediately. I don't know why these beings have to answer honestly – it doesn't make sense to me – but it seems to be a Universal Law that they do so. Please remember to use it before establishing connections with Aliens or other beings.

Can Aliens get stuck here?

I don't know what percentage of visiting Alien energies get stuck in the Earth Plane, but in my experience some do, and part of my practice is to get them unstuck and get them back to where they belong. Sometimes they don't know how to get back "home". Perhaps a homing signal is no longer operational or too distant for them to lock onto, and some are afraid to going back for fear of reprisal.

(Similarly, some dead humans are afraid of allowing their Souls to move on to their next stage of being for fear of damnation. Their Soul energies may attach to friends or family members, or places such as churches. Those are stories for another book.)

Alien Energy Survey

The following survey questions are meant to be dowsed after you have reviewed the earlier sections of the book. For your own safety and to promote the accuracy of your answers, do not begin the book here! Always begin a session by doing the Dowsing Protocol (page 31).

The questions themselves are broad and often overlapping in content. They have been written this way to create a wide net to capture knowledge, memories and experiences perhaps stored in different parts of your mind, body and energy field.

Work through these questions calmly. If you find yourself getting emotional or agitated, stop and regain your composure. Ask for the truth while you dowse, and trust yourself to handle the truth that presents itself.

You may want to work with a friend who also has dowsing skills because it's hard to dowse accurately about yourself and for things that you feel emotional about. Make sure to follow the Dowsing Protocol before beginning any of the surveys.

If you are afraid or upset:
If any of this material makes you fearful or upset, stop and take a break. You're not helping yourself or anyone else if you fall apart! Do whatever you do to bring yourself back into balance: meditate, go for a walk or talk to someone you trust. (Eating chocolate is not a solution!)

Survey 2: Am I ready to dowse safely about Alien Beings?
For safety and accuracy, dowse the following questions before dowsing any of the information in the other Surveys regarding Alien Beings. Always start with the Dowsing Protocol (page 31) to make sure are dowsing accurately. Check the **Glossary** (page 84) for definitions of terms used in the charts that you do not understand. In the charts that follow "Y" stands for "Yes" and "N" stands for "NO".

#	Y	N	Dowse: am I ready to dowse safely about Aliens?
1			Can I now dowse well enough to answer the following questions safely and accurately?
2			Should I do something else before answering these questions? (such as drink a glass of water, be better rested, be less emotional)
3			Should I dowse these questions later?
4			Should I ask someone to help me get accurate dowsing answers?
5			Do I have enough psychic protection to proceed?
6			Is my dowsing accurate? LOW MEDIUM HIGH
7			Is it best for me to now dowse the Survey I am thinking about?

If, after dowsing the survey above you do not feel ready to dowse the Alien Being surveys that follow, go back and review the chapters on Dowsing (page 29) and Psychic Protection (page 39) until you feel comfortable.

Trust your intuition to guide you as to what steps to take next. Be cautious and careful, and never take this material lightly. To the best of your ability, stay in a place of compassion and detachment, and ask for the truth. (I'd be happy to hear what you find out!) My email address is in the front pages of the book.

Survey 3: Dowse about Alien Beings
First review the questions in Survey 2 (page 62) to make sure your dowsing is safe and accurate.

#	Y	N	**Dowse about Alien Beings**
1			Are real, living, conscious Aliens visiting Earth?
2			Are objects (such as drones, robots or avatars) sent by Alien Beings visiting Earth?
3			Are there Beneficial Alien Beings? For me? For average humans? For Earth? What % of all Aliens are Beneficial?
4			Are there Nonbeneficial Alien Beings? For me? For average humans? For Earth? What % of all Aliens are Nonbeneficial?
5			Are there Neutral Alien Beings? For me? For average humans? For Earth? What % of all Aliens are Neutral?
6			Can Alien Beings change form and shapeshift?
7			Can Alien Beings look human?
8			Do Alien Beings take on the shape that I expect them to look like?
9			Can Alien Beings look like Orbs in photographs?
10			Are there Alien Beings from Off Earth living on Earth now?
11			Did Aliens from Off Earth live on Earth in the past?
12			Have any Alien Beings from another planet been born on Earth?
13			Are Alien Beings breeding with humans?
14			Were Aliens considered angels in earlier times? *Survey continues next page ...*

#	Y	N	*Survey 3 continued*
15			Were Aliens considered gods in earlier times?
16			Do Alien Beings use physical transport? While on Earth? To get to Earth?
17			Do Alien Beings use interdimensional transport? While on Earth? To get to Earth?
18			Can Alien Beings move faster than Light Speed?
19			Are Alien Beings subject to proven (by humans) laws of physics while on Earth?
20			Can Alien Beings alter Space-time?
21			Can Alien Beings time travel?
22			Do different species of Alien Beings visit Earth?
23			Did Alien Beings ever enslave humans to gather Earth resources for Alien use? Do they now?
24			Are some or all of the experiences the public has been informed of with regard to Alien Beings actually initiated by the military or other form of government?
25			Have some or all actual Alien Being encounters been covered up by the global military?

7 Dowse about You and Alien Beings

"Look up at the stars and not down at your feet. Try to make sense of what you see, and wonder about what makes the universe exist. Be curious."

Stephen Hawking

I've been communicating with inter-dimensional energies, Spirit Guides and Beneficial and Nonbeneficial Beings for years as part of my dowsing practice. I generally get good results and accurate information, and because the system was working for me, I did not ask specifically who or what I was communicating with.

That changed when I was invited to speak at a conference on Aliens. As is my habit, on my way to the conference I checked in, using the Dowsing Protocol, with the energies associated with the conference. I asked if there were beneficial Beings that I had not encountered before and who were attached to the conference, and got a *"YES"*.

But there was something about the energy that didn't "feel" quite right, so I decided to dowse a few more questions. Maintaining a neutral emotional state, I asked if any of the Beings had taken over anyone's mind and body. *"YES"*. Had they already taken over anyone's mind and body associated with the conference? *"YES"*. Did they want to take over my mind and body? *"YES"*. Were they in resonance with the *"Divine Source"*? *"NO"*. Did they accept *"Divine Holy Love"*? *"NO"*.

Through dowsing I communicated that I would not permit being taken over, and terminated the connection. This was one of the key moments when I realized that not only must we ask for Beneficial Beings, but we must ask if they are in resonance with the Divine Source. Within their own framework, these Beings that I had communicated with were beneficial, but were not beneficial to me or other humans, and by extension, the Earth.

Several months later I was on my way to attend the movie premiere of a documentary about Aliens (that I was featured in) and as before, checked in with the energies before I got there. I asked the same set of questions and received the same answers – that they wanted to take over me and others - and once again terminated the connection. To the best of my ability I then set up psychic protection for those attending the premiere.

The lessons here: don't assume that what you're communicating with is there for your own good and ask several questions to cross check answers to be sure you are communicating with beneficial energies. Chapter 9, **Initiating Contact** (page 75) gives you survey questions you can use to set up safe connections with Alien Beings.

Close Encounters

Let's look now at different types of encounters with Alien Beings so there can be a common language in the discussion.

The first three classifications of encounters, below, were developed by Allen Hynek, in his 1972 book *"The UFO Experience: A Scientific Inquiry"*. Descriptions of other kinds of encounters were later expanded by other researchers in the field and are presented below.

Table 5: Close Encounter Classifications

Kind	Experience
First kind	Detailed visual sighting of a UFO less than 500 ft (152 metres) away
Second kind	Physical effects such as equipment malfunction, trace evidence on the ground or paralysis in humans
Third kind	An animated creature is present.
Fourth kind	Abduction or experience of a transformation of reality including hallucinatory or dreamlike events.
Fifth kind	Direct communication between Alien Beings and Humans through conscious, voluntary and proactive Human-initiated cooperative communication
Sixth kind	Death of a Human or animal associated with a UFO event.
Seventh kind	Creation of a Human/Alien hybrid, either by sexual reproduction or artificial methods

People who have had an encounter and remember it, will likely experience a shift in their wold view. As long as there is no trauma associated with the memory or the experience, the person may have a sort of awakening to an expanded consciousness. If there is trauma, it can be removed through the Dowsing Protocol, Emotional Freedom Technique and/or professional counselling.

Encountering your Self as an Alien Being

In addition to the seven kinds of encounters listed above, some people feel that they themselves are an Alien Being, or are part Alien or that they have been born on Earth but belong on a different planet or in a different dimension. Perhaps some people do have past lives on other planets or by some mechanism we do not yet understand, are able to experience simultaneous lives in other dimensions or planets.

The thing to remember, is that no matter where you came from, if we are here now, we are meant to fully embody the human experience.

Survey 4: Dowse about you and Alien Beings

Think of an experience you have had, or wonder if you have had, and see if you can find out more about it using dowsing. Remember to first review the questions in Survey 2 (page 62), to make sure your dowsing is safe and accurate.

#	Y	N	Dowse about you and Alien Beings
1			Have I encountered Aliens? What type of encounter? (see page 66) How many times each? Type: 1 2 3 4 5 6 7
2			Can I communicate with Alien Beings?
3			Am I communicating with Alien Beings?
4			Have I communicated with Alien Beings in the past?
5			Will the Dowsing Protocol and other information in this book keep me safe (if I use it as directed) if I communicate with Alien Beings?
6			Is some other energy consciousness communicating with me? (See page 71) Earth? Environment? Psychic?
7			Do Aliens want to take over my mind and body? *Survey continues next page …*

#	Y	N	***Survey 4: continued***
8			Do Alien Beings want to help me in a way that will be beneficial to me from a human perspective?
9			Do Alien Beings want to help me in a way that will be nonbeneficial to me from a human perspective but beneficial to the Alien Beings?
10			Have I been abducted by Alien Beings or machines? How many times? 1-5? 6-10? More? Has this been done for my benefit?
11			Have Alien Beings or machines ever put something in me? Is it still there? How many times? 1-5? 6-10? More? Has this been done for my benefit?
12			Have any of my interactions with Alien Beings left marks on or in my body? Has this been done for my benefit?
13			Have Alien Beings ever done experiments on me? How many times? 1-5? 6-10? More? Have these been done for my benefit?
14			Have I ever met an Alien Being from Off Earth? How many times? 1-5? 6-10? More?
15			Was one of my parents an Alien Being from Off Planet? Mother? Father? (grandparents?)

Survey 5 Dowse about You and your experience

First review the questions in Survey 2 (page 62) to make sure your dowsing is safe and accurate. *Survey continues next page ..*

#	Y	N	Dowse About You and your experience
1			Am I fully Human Being?
2			Am I part Alien Being?
3			Does an Alien Being control me? Try to control me? Never Sometimes Often
4			Was I an Alien Being in a past life?
5			Is it likely I will be an Alien Being in a future life?
6			Can I choose in this life what my future Alien self will be?
7			Am I a Star Child?
8			Am I an Angel?
9			Am I a Bodhisattva?
10			Am I a Walk-in?
11			Do I come from another planet?
12			Do I come from another dimension?
13			Do I have a Soul Mission?
14			Have I made vows in this or other life times that allow Alien interactions in the life time?
15			Can I remove vows that are non-beneficial to me now using the Dowsing Protocol?
16			Can Humans alter Space-time?
17			Can I alter Space-time?
18			Do I have to report information to Alien Beings? In this lifetime?
19			Have I ever seen a UFO from off Earth ?
20			Have I ever seen a UFO from Earth?

#	Y	N	*Survey 5: continued*
21			Have I ever been on an Alien spaceship? How many times? 1-5? 6-10? More?
22			Am I living simultaneous lives? How many? On Earth? Off Earth?
23			Do I sometimes experience sleep paralysis that creates the experience of Alien interaction?
24			Has a medical condition created the experience I associate with Alien Beings?
25			Has a treatment for a medical condition created the experiences I associate with Alien Beings?
26			Are my memories of the events I associate with Alien Beings accurate? None Some All
27			Do I need more physical protection?
28			Do I need more psychic protection?
29			Is something else causing or contributing to my experience of Alien Beings? (See next chapter)

8 Dowse your other energy experiences

Encountering Non-human, Non-Alien Beings

The world is awash in conscious, non-Human, non-Alien Beings and energies. There are the obvious beings we can see and interact with on a daily basis, such as animals, and the less obvious ones that most people don't assign consciousness to, such as plants, minerals, buildings and machines. If this is a new concept for you, just act "as if" it's true and keep reading.

The work done by Cleve Baxter with plant communication is well documented in his book *"Primary Perception: Biocommunication With Plants, Living Foods and Human Cells"* (2003). In it he provides evidence that it is possible to communicate with plants and other life forms. Farmers at Findhorn in northern Scotland were some of the first westerners to begin to work with these concepts and to talk to their crops. They asked the plants where they wanted to be planted and thereby produced gigantic vegetables that continue to defy local expectations of what it is possible to grow given the soil and climate of the area.

The example above is simply meant to let you know that many things have consciousness. Some of what you may feel around you from time to time may be the energy of the earth or the environment. Not every unexplained energy phenomenon is associated with Alien presence.

Other forms of psychic consciousness that are hard to visualize, include the consciousness and energy signatures of the deceased, of past and future lives, and various thought forms. The following surveys will help you define your experiences.

Are you creating the experience?

In the chapter on consciousness (page 13) we talked about how our own resonant frequencies can potentially create a platform for Alien interaction. In the following section we will set that aside to see if there is some other energy creating the feeling you may have of personal Alien interactions.

Let's get rid of the term "Alien" for now and just call it an Energy Experience or simply Experience. Survey 6 asks you to dowse to see if you imagining these experiences or have a mental imbalance. Please don't be offended by the questions – we are casting a wide net and are searching only for your truth.

As in the other surveys, there is some overlap in the questions below which are intended to help you fine tune your answers. You may find you have inconsistent answers to some of the survey questions. Treat the information you gather as a way help you focus on future areas of study. The Dowsing Protocol can be used to resolve issues as they come up. Try creating your own survey questions to continue your personal research.

Survey 6: Dowse - I AM creating the Energy Experience
First review the questions in Survey 2 (page 62) to make sure you are safe and your dowsing is accurate.

#	Y	N	I AM creating the Energy Experience. It comes from my:
1			Memories
2			Subconscious
3			Unconscious
4			Imagination
5			Soul aspect (parts lost or need repair)
6			Higher self
7			Past life, outdated vows
8			Future life
9			Thought forms / curses (own)
10			Outdated Archetypes and survival mechanisms
11			Emotional imbalance
12			Physical imbalance
13			Spiritual imbalance
14			Mental imbalance

Survey 7: Dowse - I am NOT creating the Energy Experience

First review the questions in Survey 2 (page 62) to make sure you are safe and your dowsing is accurate.

#	Y	N	**I am NOT creating the experience** **It comes from:**
1			Collective unconscious
2			Thought forms /curses (from others)
3			Telepathy
4			Ghosts
5			Psychic cords to living or dead beings or places
6			Chakra imbalance
7			Remote viewing
8			Astral travel
9			Energy signatures
10			An aspect of my being in another dimension
11			Animal energy
12			Plant energy
13			Earth energy (Geopathic stress)
14			Environmental energy Electromagnetic, food, mould

Where does the energy experience originate?

If the experience is coming from a place outside of you, it is useful to know where it is coming from so that you can monitor it, terminate it or enhance it, depending on your intentions. The survey below will help you find that out.

The survey refers to a "standard" Universe and to standard Earth dimensions. There are many scientific theories about the structure of the universe, but we can not say for sure at this time which is correct, so when I use the term "standard", I simply mean the generally accepted model.

When I refer to standard dimensions, I am referring to the three we walk around in (height, width and length) plus time as the fourth dimension. The theoretical physics that includes String Theory currently postulates 11 dimensions, but we don't know enough to discuss them. Perhaps it is these unmapped dimensions that houses the Alien environment.

Survey 8: Dowse - where does the Energy Experience originate
First review the questions in Survey 2 (page 62) to make sure you are safe and your dowsing is accurate.

#	Y	N	Where does the Experience originate from?
1			From something in me
2			From something on the surface of the Earth
3			From something in the Earth's atmosphere
4			From something in Earth orbit
5			From something within our solar system
6			From something within our galaxy
7			From something within our standard Universe
8			From something within our standard Earth dimensions
9			From something from another dimension
10			From something related to dark energy
11			From something related to dark matter
12			From something else?

9 Initiating contact with Alien Beings

"The enemy is fear. We think it is hate; but, it is fear"
Gandhi

SAFETY WARNING!
Before attempting to initiate contact with Alien Beings,
please read the chapters on Dowsing (page 29)
and Psychic Protection (page 39).

Some people may choose to initiate and maintain contact with Beneficial Alien Beings and energies. Make sure you seek the ones that are beneficial to us as humans, who are in resonance with the Divine Source and who have useful information for you at this time.

There are Beings who can help with your Earth mission and your Soul mission. It is usually prudent to make sure your Earth mission is taken care of before, your Soul mission. This is because we need to meet our human obligations (such as caring for ourselves and our families) before we commit our resources to saving the Earth.

This may sound selfish, but if we get sick and our bodies can't function, we won't necessarily be much good at accomplishing whatever our Soul Mission is. Everyone is different of course, so make your Soul Mission as much of a priority as you sense is correct, and then make conscious choices about what your intentions are for contacting Alien Beings.

Curiosity and the desire to have a cool story to tell aren't the best motives for contact and if that's your motive, you will likely attract Nonbeneficial Beings who will promise you what you want to hear, but then take advantage of you in ways you are not prepared for.

If you are someone whose Soul Mission will benefit from direct communication with Beneficial Alien Being energies, then it is important that you have systems to do so safely. Before you begin, do the following thought experiment to be clear about what you hope to accomplish.

Box 7: Thought Experiment Two: Creating the Future

Thought Experiment Two: Creating the Future

Think about what might happen.

What do you want to happen?

What will you say?

What will do?

More techniques to manage Alien interaction

If you want to develop the ability to safely interact with Alien Beings, you need to do something to manage the process. (Please review the techniques previously listed, starting page 40)

Interact as equals

I recommend that you only seek contact with Alien Beings for a clear purpose and not out of simple curiosity or because you think it will be fun. Set up your psychic protection using the Dowsing Protocol and other techniques mentioned in the previous sections before seeking connection. Remember that it is important for you to be able to control the connection and to be able to terminate it when you choose to.

1. Do the Dowsing Protocol (page 31).

2. Indicate the purpose of your intended contact.

3. See if there are Beneficial (Alien) Beings in resonance with you and the "Divine Source" who are willing and able to assist you in fulfilling your intention and who respect your sovereign being. (Note that there are other forms of natural conscious energy that may be willing to participate.)

4. Do not proceed until the Being has agreed to cooperate within the boundaries you set.

Over time you will get a feel for the kinds of consciousness you're dealing with. Don't assume that a Being is beneficial here to help you, Humans and the Earth. Always confirm that they are with a variety of dowsing questions.

Interview with an Alien

In the questions below, it may seem odd to assume that the Being is telling the truth. Perhaps it is a Universal Law, but in my experience and in the experience of many other Dowsers, Beings do seem compelled to answer the first two questions truthfully. I was given the phrase "Divine Holy Love" by my colleague John Living many years ago, and although it is not phrasing I use in my culture, I have found it an effective filter when dealing with unknown conscious energy.

Survey 9: Determining if Beneficial or Nonbeneficial Being

First review the questions in Survey 2 (page 62) to make sure you are safe and your dowsing is accurate.

#	Y	N	Determining if Beneficial or Nonbeneficial Being
1			Are you in resonance with the Divine Source
2			Do you accept "Divine Holy Love"

If you get a NO response to the first two questions, terminate the connection immediately. If you get a YES, proceed cautiously with the following questions:

3			Are you here to help me for my benefit?
4			Are you here to help me for your benefit?
5			Are you here to help humans in general for their benefit?
6			Are you here to help humans in general for your benefit?
7			Are you here to help Earth for the Earth's benefit?
8			Are you here to help the Earth for your benefit?
9			Do you want to take over people's mind's and body's?
10			Have you taken over people's minds and body's?
11			Do you want to take over my mind and body?
12			Are you telling the truth?

If the answers to the above questions indicate the presence of a Being that is not here for your benefit or for the benefit of other humans and the Earth, or who want to take over yours our anyone's mind or body, you are obviously communicating with a Nonbeneficial Being and you should terminate the connection immediately using the Dowsing Protocol.

If after Survey 9 you are confident you are dealing with a Beneficial Being, proceed to Survey 10, below. Note that question 7 is a trick question. If the dowsing response indicates that there are non-beneficial psychic cords between you and the Being, then it may represent a danger to you. Generally speaking, non-beneficial psychic cords should always be cut.

Survey 10: Interview with a Beneficial Being
First review the questions in Survey 2 (page 62) to make sure you are safe and your dowsing is accurate.

#	Y	N	**Interview with a Beneficial Being**
1			Am I communicating with more than one Being? 0 1 2 3 4 5 6-10? More than 11? Which Being should I communicate with?
2			Can you help me with my Earth Mission?
3			Do you have information about my Earth Mission?
4			Can you help me with my Soul Mission?
5			Do you have information about my Soul Mission?
6			Are there any beneficial psychic cords between us? 0 1 2 3 4 5 6-10? More than 11? How many attached to my: Body? Mind? Soul? Emotions? Energy How many flow from me to you? How many flow from you to me?
7			Are there any nonbeneficial psychic cords between us? 0 1 2 3 4 5 6-10? More than 11?

			How many attached to my: Body? Mind? Soul? Emotions? Energy? How many flow from me to you? How many flow from you to me?
			Have we had a relationship in other lifetimes? 1 2 3 4 5 6-10? More than 11?
			How many times in the past have we been: Family: mother father son daughter sister brother Friends? Enemies? Masters? Slaves? Other?
			Can you help me facilitate my health: Physically? Emotionally? Spiritually? Mentally? Energetically? Financially?

Helping Beneficial Beings

Sometimes a Being that needs your help presents itself. Survey 11 can help you determine if this is the case. In some cases a Being may need help getting *"home"*. I use the word here to mean *"where it belongs"* because most Beings seem to recognize that as a concept.

Based on the information you uncover in Survey 11, you may need to dowse further questions to determine precisely what is needed. To give a non Alien example, I once helped a deceased male spirit get "home". He indicated he didn't want to go because he was waiting for his spouse so that they could go together. When I checked for her energy, I found she had been deceased for twenty years and had already left! I let the fellow know, then asked, with dowsing, if he was ready to go now. He indicated *"YES"*, and I asked Beneficial Beings to help him get there.

This may all sound quite complicated, but with practice and asking the right questions, things just seem to fall into place if you take your time and follow the methods described in the Dowsing Protocol.

Survey 11: Can you help the Beneficial Being

First review the questions in Survey 2 (page 62) to make sure you are safe and your dowsing is accurate.

xx	Y	N	Can you help the Beneficial Being
			Can I be of assistance to you? To get home? With forgiveness? With something else?
			If YES for getting home: Do you know how to get Home?
			Do you have what you need to get Home?
			Do you have to do something before you go Home?
			Is there something you need to communicate before you go Home?
			Are there one or more Beings you need to communicate with before you go Home? Human (living/dead) 1-5 6-10 more than: 10, 100, 1000 Animal (living/dead) 1-5 6-10 more than: 10, 100, 1000 Alien (living/dead) 1-5 6-10 more than: 10, 100, 1000
			If YES for forgiveness: Do you need to ask for forgiveness? Ask me for forgiveness? Me this lifetime? Past? Future? Ask someone else? This lifetime? Past? Future?
			Do you need to forgive someone or something? Forgive me? Me this lifetime? Past? Future? Forgive someone else? This lifetime? Past? Future?

10 Conclusion

"On the return trip home, gazing through space toward the stars and the planet from which I had come, I suddenly experienced the universe as intelligent, loving, harmonious."   Edgar Mitchell
NASA Astronaut, Apollo 14

It seems likely that there is currently some form of Alien presence on Earth, whether it exists as humanoid creatures that live among us, or as subtle electromagnetic energies that we can detect with specialized tools and awareness, it is already here.

We don't know what our future is with Alien Beings on this planet, but we can create it. Each of us in the best way possible, must choose between two paths. One is the path of denial, fear, and destruction. We could easily blow up our planet through ignorance and intolerance of those different from ourselves. The other path is one of intelligent action that embraces not only all humanity as being related, but also accepts the "Being-ness" of Alien Beings.

This is the time and place where you get to choose what the rest of your life will be like. Create a vision of it; choose it, then take action as if it is possible to achieve it. Over time, you will achieve what you set out to do. Call on help from Beneficial Beings who are in resonance with the Divine Source (call them Aliens or Angels or whatever feels right).

Even if you're not sure if the techniques to manage interactions with Alien Beings presented in this book are working, act as if they are. Check and adjust your energies regularly using the Dowsing Protocol. Go back and do the surveys once in a while to see if the answers have changed. Do and share your own research.

There are universal laws that guide us: to show respect for one another, to manage our bodies, our planet, and our universe in ways that will be sustainable for all time.

Together we may be able to bring the best of our worlds together, and perhaps someday our culture will also be seeded in the stars.

Appendix: Preliminary Survey Results

This is a new book (June 2016) and the surveys listed in Chapters 6 to 9 have not been available long enough to have a large number of people complete them. I presented them, in modified form, as part of a dowsing workshop. Attendees, some of whom were beginners, were invited to complete them. The results below are what a small group of trained Dowsers found to be true for them. The results are not presented as statistics.

As I workshop this material with other trained Dowsers, I will update the survey results in this book. I also invite you to send me your responses and I will keep track of them (anonymously) as well and include the aggregate results in future editions.

What surprised me about the answers, is how consistent the group was. There was about ninety percent agreement for most questions.

Subject line: "Results"
Send me your results and I'll include them in future editions of this book (without using your name of course).   susan@dowser.ca

Survey 3: Dowse about Alien Beings Results
About 90% of the group dowsed that:
- there are real, living Alien Beings visiting and living on Earth as well as drones, robots or avatars sent by Alien Beings;
- both Beneficial and Nonbeneficial Alien Beings are visiting the Earth (about 60% found that Neutral Alien Beings are visiting);
- Alien Beings can shapeshift and look human (about 75% found they do not have consistent form);
- That Alien Beings use both physical and inter-dimensional transport (the question didn't ask, but we can presume they use physical transport while on Earth and inter-dimensional transport getting here and away);
- Aliens can move faster than the speed of light, can alter Space-time and time travel'
- Aliens are breeding with humans.

Survey 4: Dowse about You and Alien Beings Results
About 90% of the group dowsed that:
- they could communicate with Aliens, and had done so in the past and about 60% found that they were communicating now. There

was an also a strong agreement that some *other consciousness is communicating with me*";

- Aliens want to help me in a way that is nonbeneficial to me from a human perspective but beneficial to them. (Only 50% found Aliens wanted to help them from a human perspective);
- they had not been abducted by Aliens, nor had experiments been done them. (About 50% found they had met an Alien Being and that something had been put in them);
- one of their parents was NOT an Alien.

Survey 5: Dowse about You and your energy experience Results

People dowsed that:

- 90% were neither Star Children nor Walk-Ins; nor did they experience Sleep Paralysis; that they were Bodhisattvas;
- about half found: they came from another planet; had seen a UFO on Earth; were living simultaneous lives; that their memories were accurate;
- All had a Soul Mission, but none had to report information back to Alien Beings.

Survey Summary

Although the survey results presented here are not statistically meaningful, and these early versions of the questions can be fine tuned to extract more information, it is interesting to see there is a strong trend towards the idea that Alien Beings are visiting Earth and helping humans not in ways that are beneficial to humans but that are beneficial to the Alien Beings! Should we be afraid! No - we need to be aware and to take steps to have psychic protection so that we can always maintain control over our experiences.

Glossary

Abductee: someone who has been taken under the control of Aliens.

Akashic Records: (Sanskrit) idea that information is recorded in the astral plane and can be recalled.

Alien Being: a Being who is not native to Earth.

Angel: a Being believe to be a messenger of God.

Animal energy: energy of animals that may be conscious.

Astral plane: idea that there is a place between earth and heaven the soul can visit.

Astral Travel: idea that aspects of our Self can travel to the Astral Plane to access information

Avatar: a figure representing a deity or controlling mind

Beings of the Universe: phrase used by Pope Francis that some interpret as referring to Alien Beings.

Big Bang: the rapid expansion of matter at the origin of the universe.

Bodhisattva: an enlightened being who remains incarnated to help others.

Collective Unconscious: (Carl Jung) shared aspects of the unconscious mind such as instincts, archetypes and symbols.

Conscious mind: things inside our normal awareness.

Contactee: a person who has been contacted by Alien Beings.

Dark Energy: an unknown matter making up 27% of the universe.

Dark Matter: an unknown energy making up 68% of the universe.

Déjà vu: the feeling of having already experienced current events.

Dimension: a measurement in physical space.

Divine Source: the essential source of beneficial energy and creation.

"Divine Holy Love": if a Being accepts this, it is likely beneficial.

Dowsing: the detection and transformation of subtle energy, often with tools and the power of heart and thought.

Dowsing Protocol: a way of accurately accessing your natural intuition **while Dowsing.**

Earth Energies: various energy systems in the earth, such as magnetic and electromagnetic that may be conscious.

Earth Faults: provide a pathway for underground water flow.

Electromagnetic energy: having both electric and magnetic characteristics.

Energy Field: region of electric, gravitational, magnetic etc. influence.

Energy matrix: a system of automatically creating energy conditions.

Energy phenomena: events and manifestations that have no conventional explanation.

Energy signature: the residue energy left over from an event or person.

ETs Extraterrestrials: Beings not from Earth.

Exoplanet: a planet that orbits a star outside our solar system.

Experiencer: Someone who has had an experience of Alien phenomena.

Frequency: how often an energy wave repeats in a measure of time. Measured in Hertz (Hz) or Cycles per Second (CPS).

Future Life: a period of time in the current or future body.

Geomancy: the art of designing and placing structures in the landscape so that the Earth Energies enhance their intended use, and so that the structure itself is in harmony with the environment. Similar to Feng Shui.

Geopathic Stress: the impact of non-beneficial earth energies on living organisms.

Ghost: an active energy of a dead being that has not transitioned to its next phase of development.

god: also deity. A being worshipped as having power.

God: the creator and ruler of the universe in monotheistic religions.

God Helmet: also Koren Helmet. A device that manipulates electromagnetic frequencies which may create paranormal experiences.

Guides: a Being that shows the way to others.

Hertz: Hz. Cycles Per Second (CPS). Used to describe frequency.

Hive Mind: Beings that think alike and do not tolerate challenges.

Home: the place a Being belongs and generally wants to get back to.

Imagination: visualization of new things and ideas.

Incarnation: the body that the **Self** inhabits in a lifetime.

Higher Self: an unconscious, subconscious or super-conscious version of oneself.

Interdimensional Transport: the ability to move through Space-time and between dimensions in ways that are not currently understood.

Karma: the sum of one's previous actions determine their future.

Law of attraction: like attracts like.

Light year: the distance light travels in a year. (about 6 trillion miles

Lives in other dimensions: a sense some people have of living on Earth and elsewhere at the same time.

Lucid dreaming: the dreamer is aware that they are dreaming.

Magnetic Anomaly: area with unusual magnetic characteristics.

Magnetic Images: false readings of earth energies due to magnetic deflection.

Map Dowsing: using a map to remotely detect the location of something.
Memory: the ability of the mind to retrieve stored information.
Metaphysics: the study of the nature of reality.
Milky Way: the galaxy to which our sun belongs.
Mineral energy: energy of minerals that may be conscious.
Negative: (-) refers to the electrical charge of an object. Does NOT mean non-beneficial energy.
Nonhuman based: not originating from a human.
Off-Earth: Matter outside of the Earth atmosphere.
Orbs: energy phenomena commonly photographed that may represent conscious energy.
Paranormal: phenomena that are beyond the scope of normal scientific understanding.
Past Life: a period of time in the current or previous body.
Piezoelectric: the electric charge that builds in materials such as crystal, bone, and DNA in response to mechanical stress.
Plant Energy: energy of plants that may be conscious.
Polarity: the electrical charge or condition of a body. Positive (+) or negative (-).
Poltergeist: a supernatural Being that can create physical disturbances.
Portal: a gateway. In this book, between dimensions.
Positive: (+) refers to the electrical charge of an object. Does NOT refer to beneficial energy.
Preconscious mind: information that can be retrieved by the **Conscious Mind.**
Psychic Cord: a draining energy flow between people.
Quantum wave: the description of all the probable states of a system.
Quantum entanglement: groups of particles that must be described together. What acts on one, acts on all.
Quantum possibilities: all the possible states of a system.
Radiation: the energy transfer of electromagnetic waves from, for example, moving water.
Rays: lines of energy.
Remote Sensing: detection at a distance.
Remote viewing: the ability to mentally view places without being there physically.
Resonance: responding to vibrations of a particular frequency, especially by itself vibrating.
Self: the individual identity of the Soul.
Shape Shifting: the ability to change physical form.

Sleep Paralysis: a transitional state between waking and sleeping where the mind is conscious but the body is immobile.

Soul: the essence of Self which persists through time.

Soul Aspect: a part of the Soul that may be splintered from the whole due to trauma or other circumstance.

Soul Mission: the purpose of the Self.

Space-time: the concept of time and three-dimensional space regarded as fused in a four-dimensional continuum.

Spirit of Place / Genius Loci: In Roman mythology a *genius loci* was the protective spirit of a place.

Standard Universe: the universe we recognize as our own.

Star Child: a **Soul** originating beyond Earth and experience simultaneously in many realities, timelines, and realms.

String Theory: theory of quantum physics. See page 24.

Subconscious mind: existing in the mind but not consciously known or felt. Unconscious mind.

Subconscious Self: the Self that controls many emotions, actions and reactions.

Subtle energy: energies not easily detected by standard tools.

Super conscious mind: transcending human consciousness

Telepathy: the ability of one or more people to communicate at a distance.

Thought Form: an energy pattern produced by thoughts or emotions that can remain as an imprint at the location.

UFO: Unidentified Flying Object often associated with **Extraterrestrial** spacecraft.

Uncanny valley: a humanoid figure closely resembling a human, but which arouses a sense of unease in the viewer.

Unconscious Mind: mental processes the individual is unaware of.

Universal Laws: laws taught by the majority of wisdom traditions governing conduct that include don't lie, don't steal and be kind to each other.

Vibration: rapid motion to and fro of an electro-magnetic wave.

Walk-in: a being originating in another dimension or Space-time who visits the Earth, generally by taking over an existing physical being.

Wavelength: distance from the crest of one wave to the next.

Wi-Fi: a wireless, local network for transmitting electromagnetic signals.

Witness: a sample of an object being sought by dowsing.

Bibliography

Books

Baxter, Cleve. *Primary Perception: Biocommunication With Plants, Living Foods and Human Cells.* Anza, CA: White Rose Millennium Press, 2003

Bowler and Morus. *Making Modern Science.* Chicago: University of Chicago Press, 2005.

Clark, Arthur. *Profiles of the Future.* New York Warner Books,1985

Collins, Susan. *Bridge Matter and Spirit with Dowsing.* King City, ON: Collins, 2006.

______. *Dowsing Triage – Finding and Fixing Energy Problems.* King City, ON: Collins, 2010.

______. *Get Happy with Dowsing.* King City, ON: Collins, 2011.

______. *Meeting Orbs in Sacred Space.* King City, Collins, 2008.

Donderi, Dan. *UFOs, ETs, and Alien Abductions.* Charlottesville, VA: Hampton Roads, 2013

Freud, Sigmund. *A General Introduction to Psychoanalysis.* New York: Simon and Schuster, 1970.

Hawkings, Steven. *A Brief History of Time.* New York, Bantam Books, 1988.

Hynek, J. Allen. *The UFO Experience: A Scientific Inquiry.* London: Corgi Books, 1972

Kaku, Michio. *Physics of the Impossible.* NewYork: Doubleday, 2008

Kahneman, Daniel. *Thinking, Fast and Slow.* New York: Farrar, 2011

McTaggart, Lynne. *The Field.* New York: Harper, 2008.

Quitt, Jason. *Forbidden Knowledge.* Seattle: Createspace, 2016.

Wald, Robert. *Space, Time and Gravity.* Chicago: University of Chicago Press, 1977

Websites

Gary Craig: *www.emofree.com*

National Aeronautics and Space Administration: *www.nasa.gov*

Wikipedia: *https://en.wikipedia.org*

First People – The Legends *www.firstpeople.us/FP-Html-Legends/AlgonandtheSkyGirl-Algonquin.html*

Video

Marconi, Lana. *The Resonance.* 2015. *drlana.com/blog/index.php/the-resonance-film/*

Susan Collins

Personal Management Consultant
Professional Dowser

The Canadian Society of Dowsers
President, 2003 -2006
Dowser of the Year, 2006

Presenter at National Conferences

Alien Cosmic Expo, Brantford, ON, Canada
American Society of Dowsers Conference, Lyndonville, Vermont, USA
ASD West Coast Convention, Santa Cruz, California, USA
ASD Southwest Conference, Flagstaff, Arizona, USA
Binnaji General Trading Co, Kuwait City, Kuwait
British Society of Dowsers Conference, Cirencester and Leicester, UK
Canadian Society of Dowsers Conference, Toronto, London,
    Peterborough, ON, Canada
CanAm 1, ASD/CSQ Conference, Harrison Hot Springs, BC Canada
Questers Conferences:100 Mile House and Salmon Arm, BC and Olds,
    Alta Canada
Foundation of Mind Being Research, Palo Alto, California, USA
Italian Dowsing Society, Bologna, Italy
Ozark Research Institute Conference, Fayetteville, Arkansas, USA
Plus, many regional meetings and events across North America

Author: Books

Bridge Matter and Spirit with Dowsing
Dowsing for Feng Shui and Space Clearing
Meet Alien Energy with Dowsing

Dowsing That Works Series

Use a Protocol to Get Results Classic, Bible, Muslim editions
Dowsing Triage – Finding and Fixing Energy Problems
Meeting Orbs in Sacred Space
Water Wells – What a Dowser Needs to Know
Get Happy with Dowsing – Change Unhealthy Patterns

Publications

What's New in Dowsing – CSD quarterly journal, Canada
The Quester – CSQ/CSD quarterly journal, Canada
The American Dowser – ASD Quarterly Digest, USA
Dowsing Today – British Society of Dowsers, U.K.
Journal- The Dowsing Society of New South Wales, Australia,
Revista Cientifica Radiestesia – Dowsing Society of Chile
Human Spirit Magazine – Ontario, Canada
Vitality Magazine, KI Awareness – Ontario, Canada

Film

Resonance Film *drlana.com/blog/index.php/the-resonance-film/*

Television

City TV; Rogers TV; VRLand News.

Other books by Susan Collins
available from www.dowser.ca and Amazon

Left to right from top row: Bridge Matter and Spirit with Dowsing; Dowsing for Feng Shui and Space Clearing; Meeting Orbs in Sacred Space; Use a Protocol to Get Results (Classic, Bible and Muslim Editions); Dowsing Triage – Finding and Fixing Energy Problems; Get Happy with Dowsing – Change Unhealthy Patterns and Water Wells – What a Dowser Needs to Know.

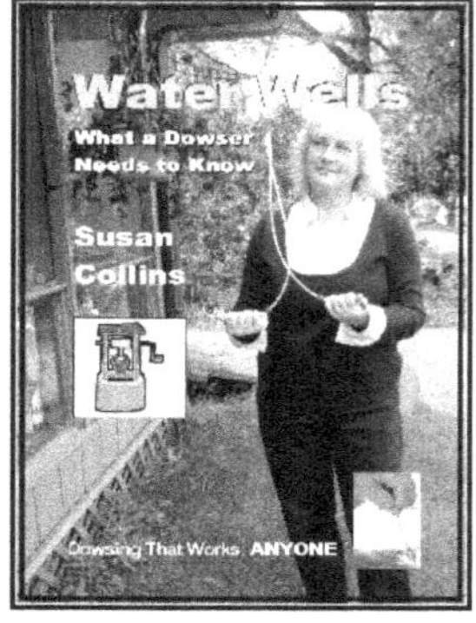